Alan Turing's Number Puzzles For Kids

This edition published in 2023 by Arcturus Publishing Limited
26/27 Bickels Yard, 151–153 Bermondsey Street,
London SE1 3HA

Puzzles by Puzzle Press

Author: Eric Saunders
Illustrator: Eve O'Brien
Illustrations on the following page are from Shutterstock: 66.
Editor: Lydia Halliday

CH010498NT
Supplier 10, Date 0723, PI0004109

Printed in the UK

Sudoku Fours

Fill the empty squares in each grid, so that there is one of every number in each row, column, and mini-grid of four squares. The numbers to use are 1, 2, 3, and 4.

	3	4	
2			
			1

2			
		1	
	3		
		4	

			1
2			
			3
4			

		4	
3			
2		1	

Numberlink

Travel from circle to circle in any direction along the lines to find the sequence 1-2-3-4-5, which appears once only.

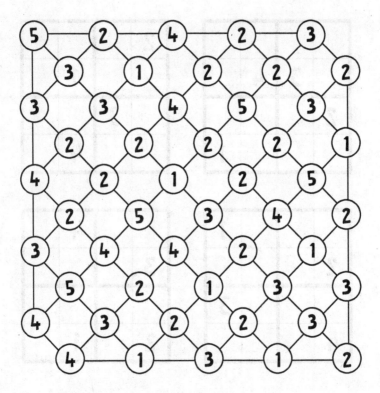

5 2 4 2 3
3 1 2 2 2
3 3 4 5 3
2 2 2 2 1
4 2 1 2 5
2 5 3 4 2
3 4 4 2 1
5 2 1 3 3
4 3 2 2 3
4 1 3 1 2

Sequences

Follow each of these sequences from the circle at the top. What number should be in the central circle of each diagram?

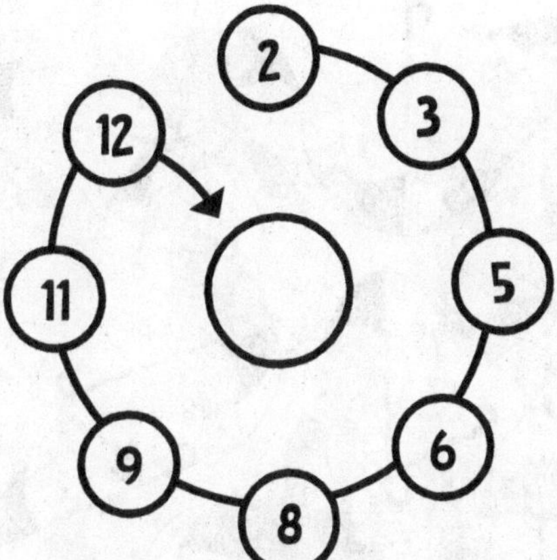

2, 3, 5, 6, 8, 9, 11, 12, ?

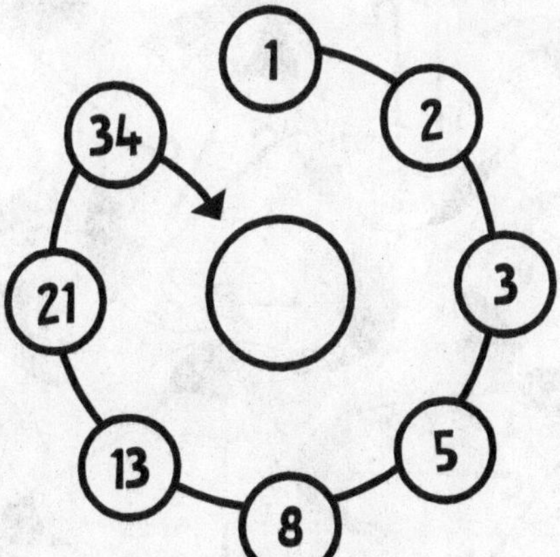

1, 2, 3, 5, 8, 13, 21, 34, ?

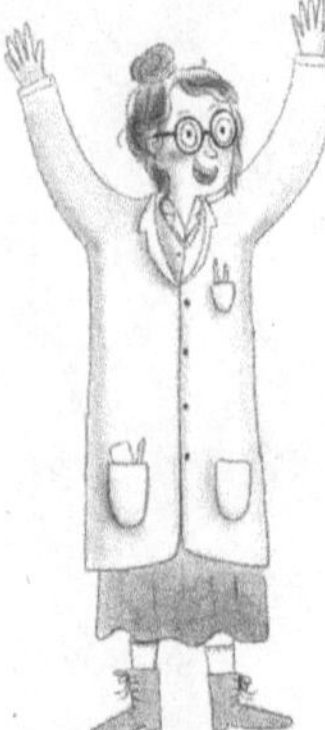

Umbrellas

How many umbrellas can you see?

How many whole numbers divide exactly into that number?

X Numbers

Fill the X shape with the listed numbers, one digit per square. All numbers are used just once, and one is already in place.

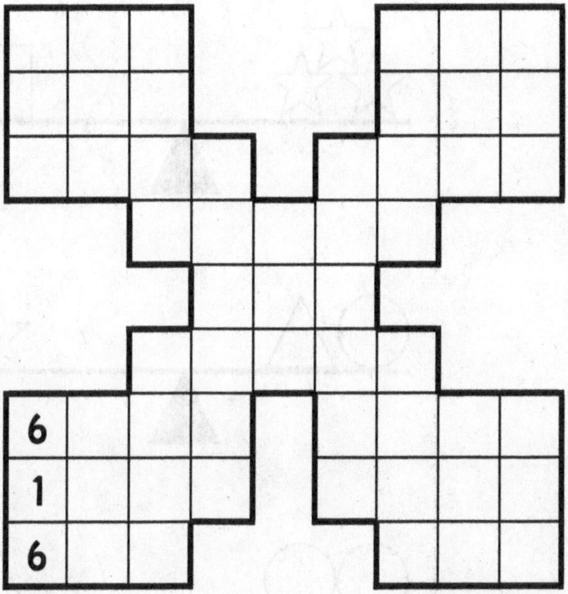

6								
1								
6								

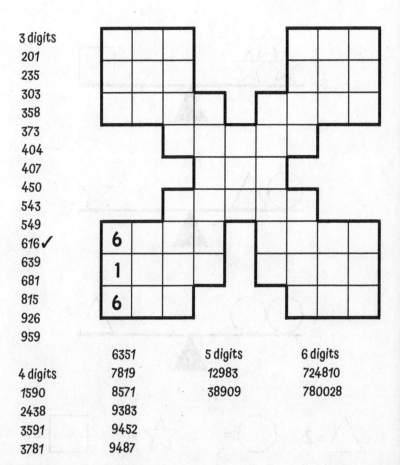

3 digits
201
235
303
358
373
404
407
450
543
549
616✓
639
681
815
926
959

4 digits
1590
2438
3591
3781
6351
7819
8571
9383
9452
9487

5 digits
12983
38909

6 digits
724810
780028

Balancing Act

All of the scales below are perfectly balanced. If the triangle weighs 2, what do the other shapes weigh?

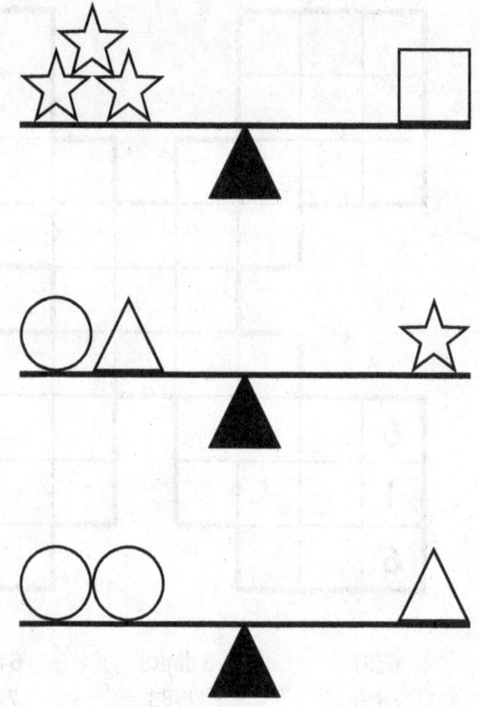

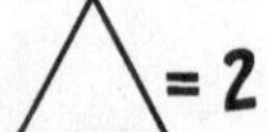

 =

 =

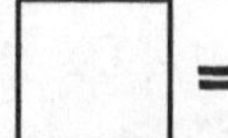 =

Spot the Dots!

Some circles in this puzzle are already black. Shade in more circles, so that the quantity of black circles totals the number inside the area they surround.

Every black circle with a number higher than 1 needs to be next to another black circle surrounding the same area. When solving, it may help to put a small dot in any circle that you know should not be filled.

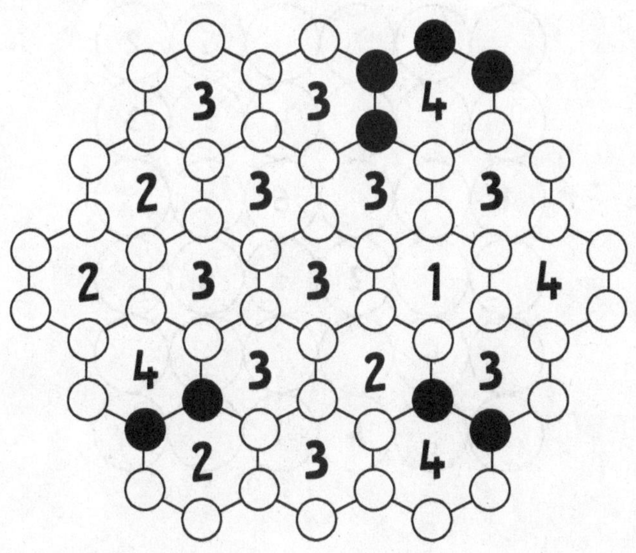

Round Numbers

Fill the empty circles, so that every horizontal row and vertical column of six circles contains the numbers 1 to 6. The shaded circles should contain odd numbers 1, 3, and 5, and the white circles should contain even numbers 2, 4, and 6. Some numbers are already in place.

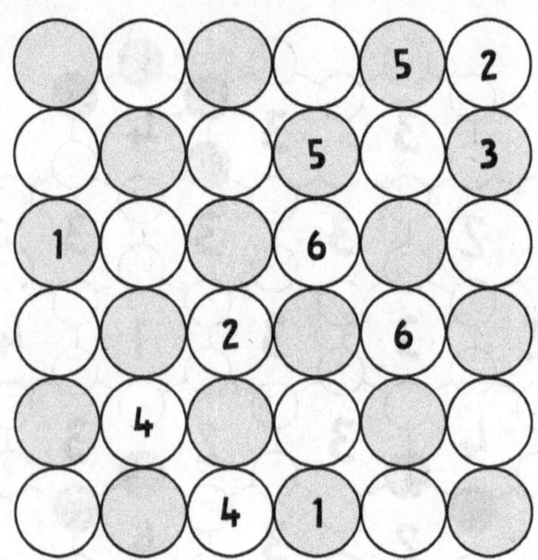

Brickwork

Fill each empty square with a single-digit number from 1 to 8. No number may appear twice in any row or column. In any set of two squares separated by dotted lines, one square contains an odd number, and the other contains an even number.

		2		5		1	6
	2	3	4				8
		1	6	3		5	
8	1		5			3	7
4		7			1		
7		5	1			8	2
	4		3		7	2	
6				7	5	4	

Chains

Write the numbers 1 to 5 in the empty circles below, so that the numbers appear just once in every row, column, and connected set of five circles.

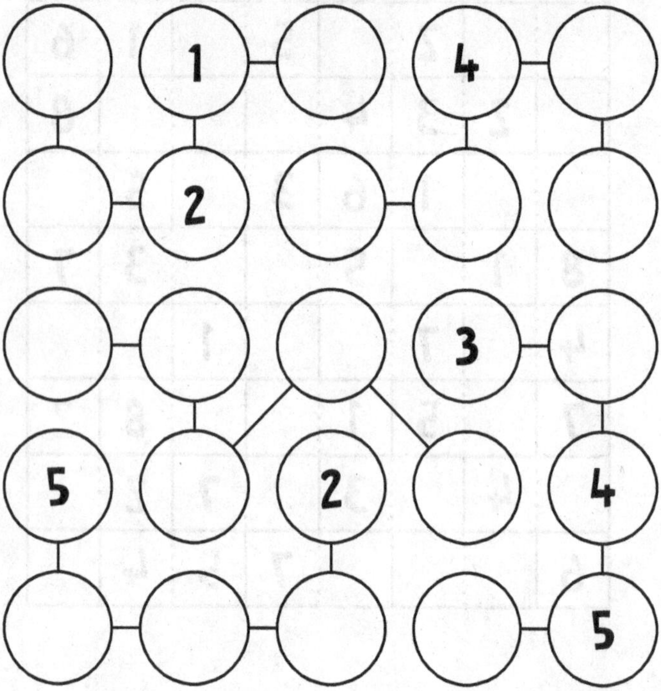

	1		4	
	2			
			3	
5		2		4
				5

Borders

Divide this grid into rectangles, each containing a single number. The number in each rectangle must match the number of squares enclosed by it. Don't forget that squares are rectangles too! One has been done for you.

	6	2		1	
				6	3
			4		
	3				
2			2		
1	4				
		3	1		4

Zigzag

Draw a single path from the top left square to the bottom right square of the grid, moving through all of the squares in either a horizontal, vertical, or diagonal direction. Lines should only pass through a square once, and your path should take you through the numbers in the sequence 1-2-3-4-1-2-3-4, etc. Can you find the way through?

1	3	4	1
3	2	2	2
4	1	1	3
2	3	4	4

Circle Games

The number in each circle is the total of the numbers in the two touching circles below it. For each blank circle, fill in the missing number.

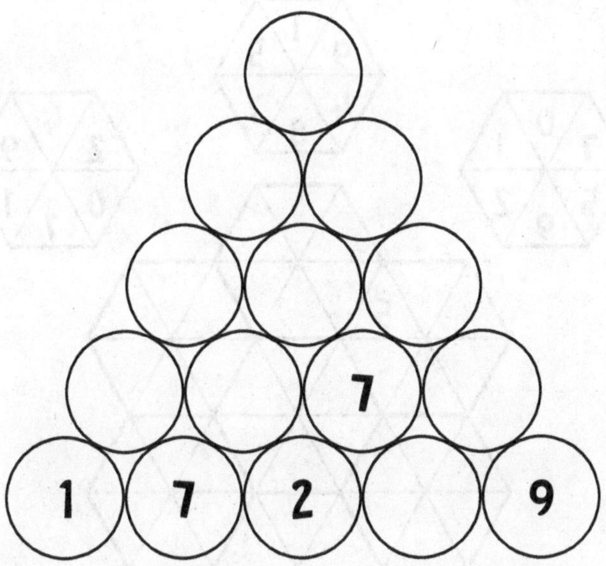

Hexagony

Can you place the hexagons into the grid, so that where any hexagon touches another along a straight line, the number in both triangles is the same? No rotation of any hexagon is allowed! One number is already in place.

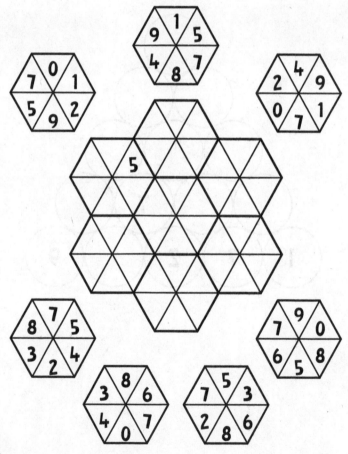

9 1 5
4 8 7

7 0 1
5 9 2

2 4 9
0 7 1

5

8 7 5
3 2 4

7 9 0
6 5 8

3 8 6
4 0 7

7 5 3
2 8 6

Picture Perfect

Shade in all dominoes that have two halves with dots that add up to an even number (for example: 0:2 = 2, 2:2 = 4, and 3:5 = 8). Your shading will reveal a picture.

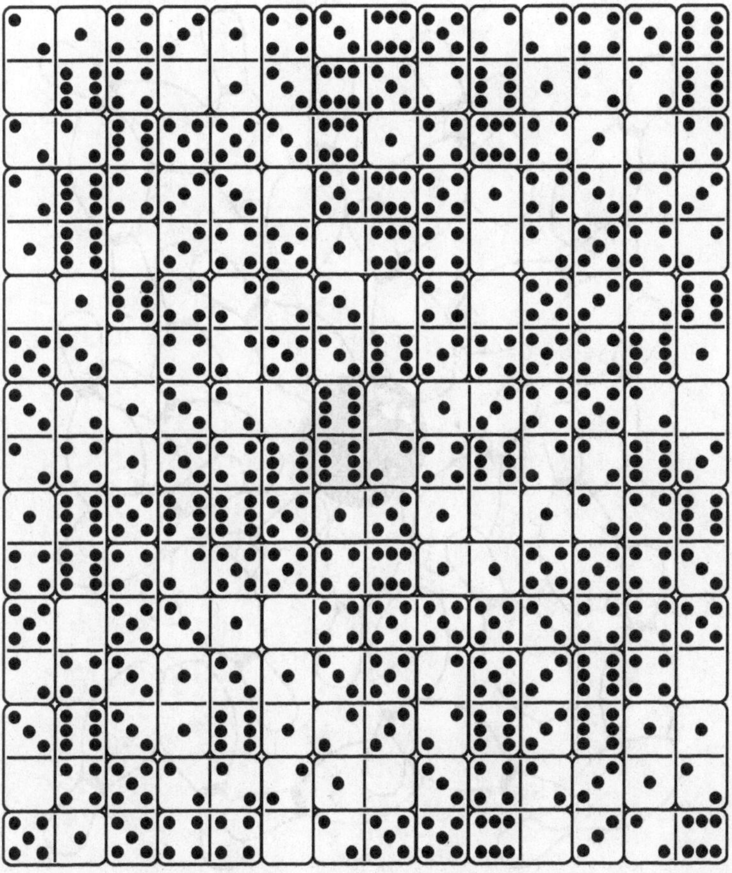

Bowled Over

How many bowling pins can you count in this picture? How many whole numbers divide exactly into that number?

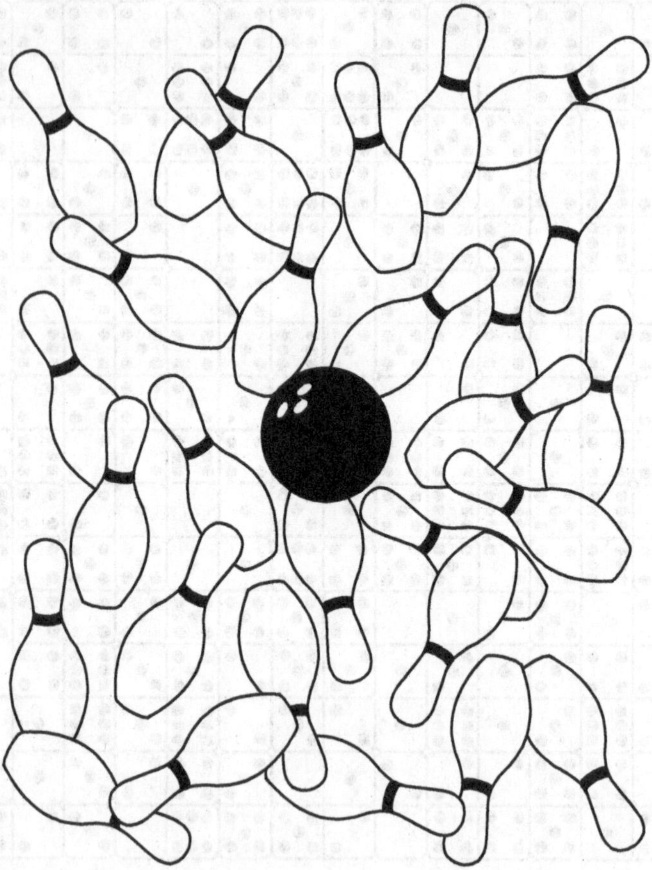

Number-Hunting

You will need good eyesight and concentration to find the listed numbers in this puzzle. They can run backward or forward, in either a horizontal, vertical, or diagonal direction.

0	9	3	9	1	8	2	3	1	8
9	5	2	3	2	0	9	8	5	7
9	7	1	8	3	1	3	0	7	1
4	0	1	1	3	5	4	6	6	8
0	6	6	3	7	1	4	4	9	8
6	9	2	1	0	5	1	9	2	9
7	3	1	6	2	1	1	4	2	8
7	4	6	5	8	7	4	5	3	7
7	4	0	8	4	4	7	3	1	0
5	6	5	4	5	5	6	1	8	3

1885
25467
283114
4129
45561
513

71150
7199
741175
819
9857
9940677

Hexafit

Can you place these numbers in the hexagons? They need to be entered in a clockwise direction around each lettered hexagon. One number is already in position; cross off the others as you use them.

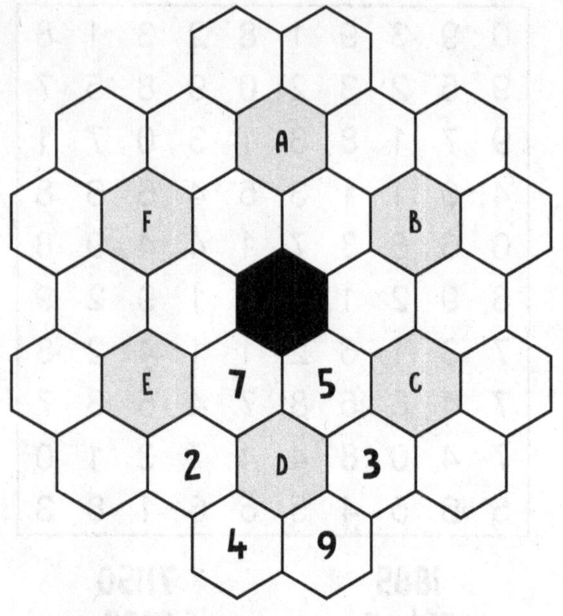

~~275394~~ 587261

379854 697425

423579 839765

Flower Power

Without rotating any, find the matching pairs of flowers, then multiply the numbers in the middle of each pair. What are the answers? Are any answers exactly the same?

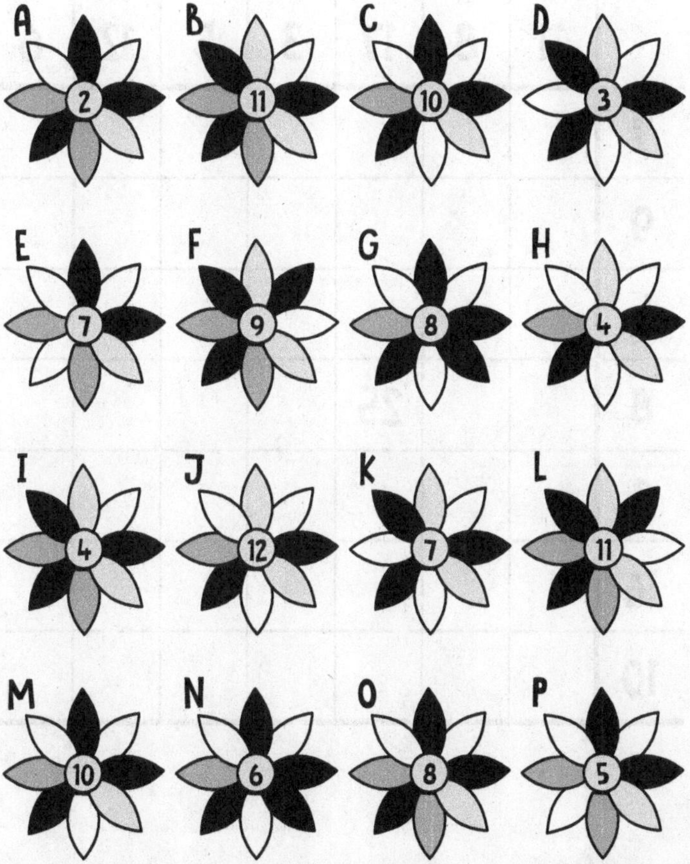

A 2 B 11 C 10 D 3

E 7 F 9 G 8 H 4

I 4 J 12 K 7 L 11

M 10 N 6 O 8 P 5

Cross-Referencing

Cross-reference the numbers in the horizontal rows and vertical columns of the grid below, and calculate the totals when the two numbers are added together.

One has already been done as an example: 8 + 17 = 25.

	11	8	17	3	5	12	6
7							
9							
4							
8			25				
2							
16							
10							

Sudoku Sixes

Fill the empty squares in each grid, so that there is one of every number in each row, column, and mini-grid of six squares. The numbers to use are 1, 2, 3, 4, 5, and 6.

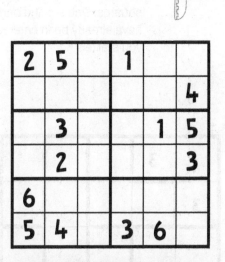

2	5		1		
					4
	3			1	5
	2				3
6					
5	4		3	6	

4		2			
				5	
5			1		6
	2			3	
					1
6		3			5

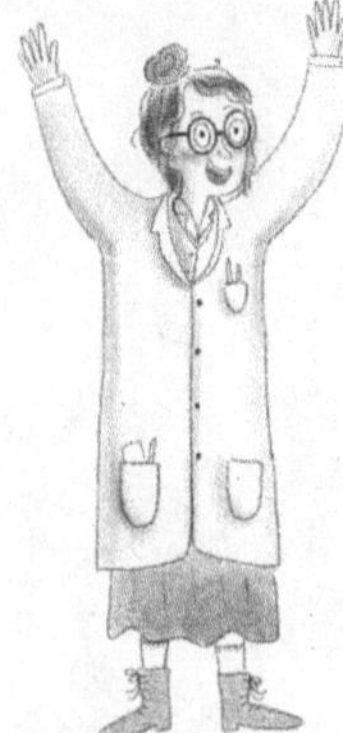

Five Square

Place a number from 1 to 5 into each empty square, so that when the numbers in each heavily outlined shape are added together, they equal the small number in the top left corner. No number may appear twice in any horizontal row or vertical column of five squares. One set and one extra number have already been entered, to get you started.

7 **1**	**3**	10	12	6
3				
7		7		12
3			**4**	
11				

Three Dice

Can you find three dice that have exactly the same total number of dots on the faces you can see?

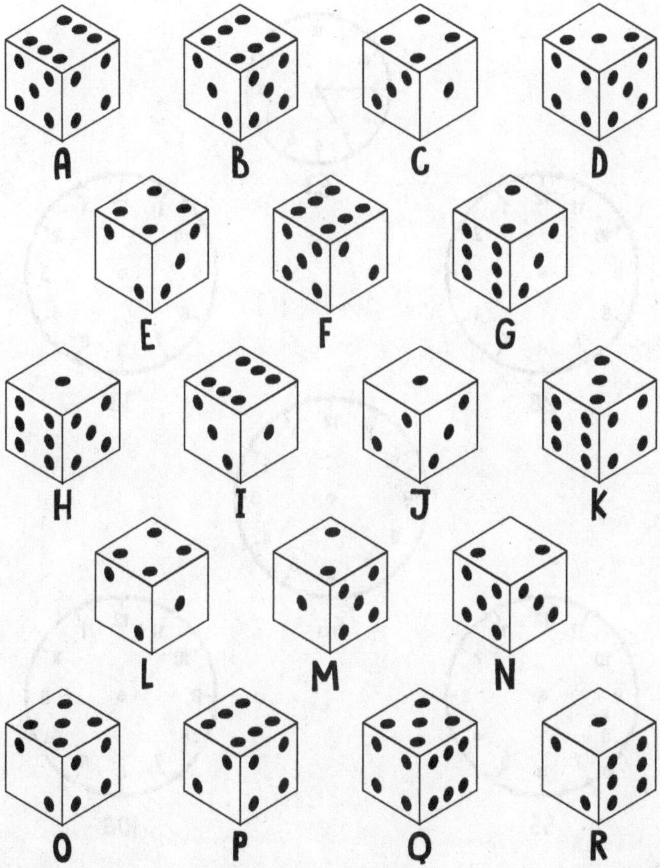

A B C D

E F G

H I J K

L M N

O P Q R

Multiplication Times

Draw in the hands on these clocks, so that when the numbers the hands point to are multiplied together, they equal the number below the clock. Use the hour hand (shortest) for the lowest number, and the minute hand (longest) for the highest number, like the example.

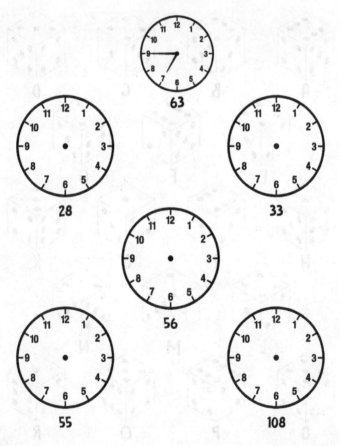

63

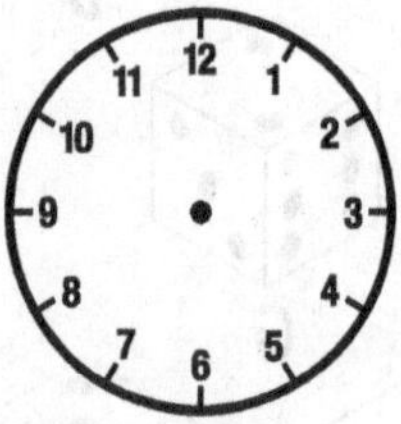

28

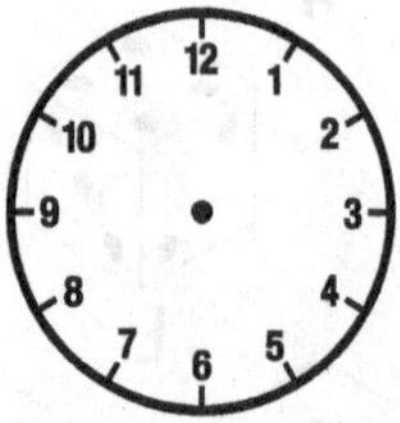

33

56

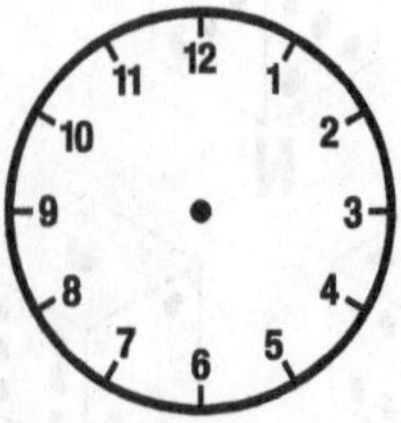

55

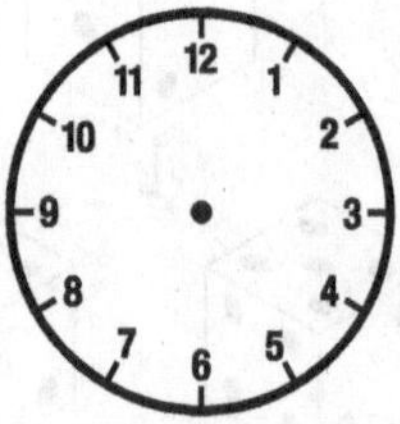

108

Eight High

Complete this number pyramid, so that every brick is filled with a number from 1 to 9 that is either the total of the two numbers in the two bricks below it, or the difference between the numbers in those two bricks, like this:

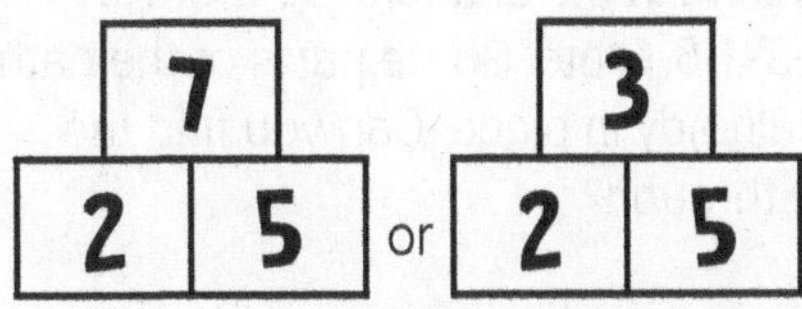

The numbers in each row must all be different.

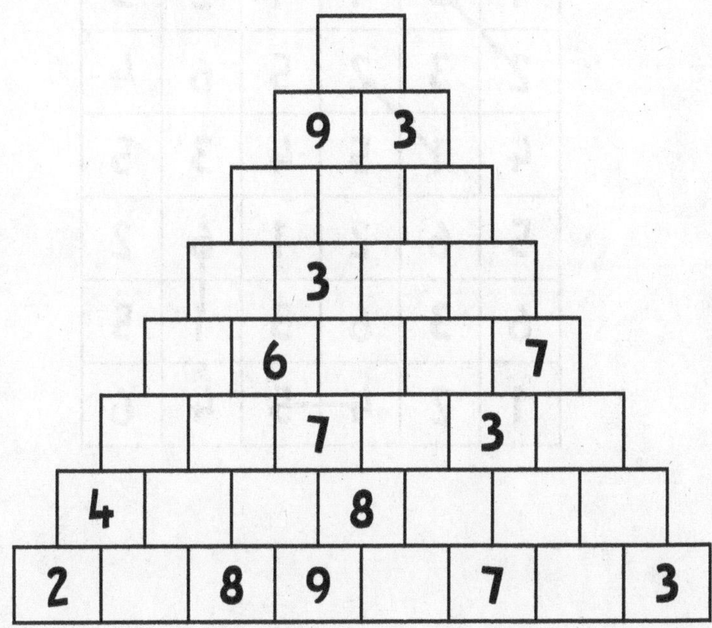

Pathfinder

Draw a single path from the top left square to the bottom right square of the grid, moving through all of the squares in either a horizontal, vertical, or diagonal direction. Lines should only pass through a square once, and your path should take you through the numbers in the sequence 1-2-3-4-5-6-1-2-3-4-5-6, etc. Some parts of the path are already in place. Can you find the way through?

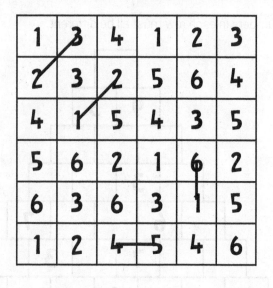

1	3	4	1	2	3
2	3	2	5	6	4
4	1	5	4	3	5
5	6	2	1	6	2
6	3	6	3	1	5
1	2	4	5	4	6

Running Totals

Five children (Amelia, Ben, Claire, Dylan, and Elijah) are in training for their school's half-marathon. Each ran for various numbers of miles every day from Monday to Friday last week.

The distance in miles is to the left of the graph below, and the initial letter of each child's name is to the right.

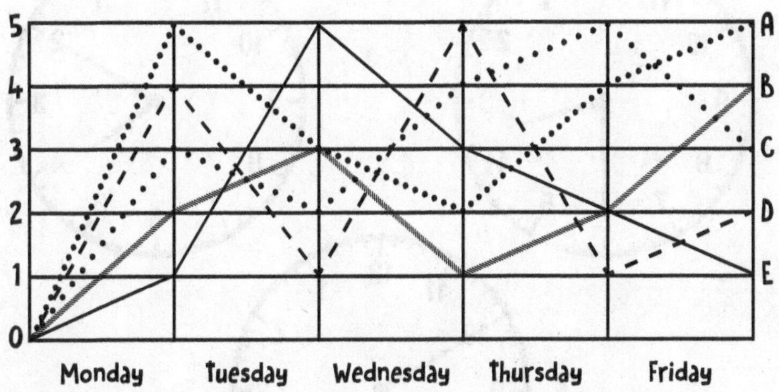

1. Who ran the longest distance in total last week?
2. Who ran the shortest distance from Monday to Wednesday?
3. How many children ran fewer miles on Tuesday than on Monday?
4. Which children ran the same distance on Friday as they had run on Monday?
5. Which children ran for a total of six miles on Wednesday and Thursday?

Clockwork

Work out the time differences between the four clocks, reading them in the order 1, 2, 3, and 4, then draw the missing hands on the fifth clock.

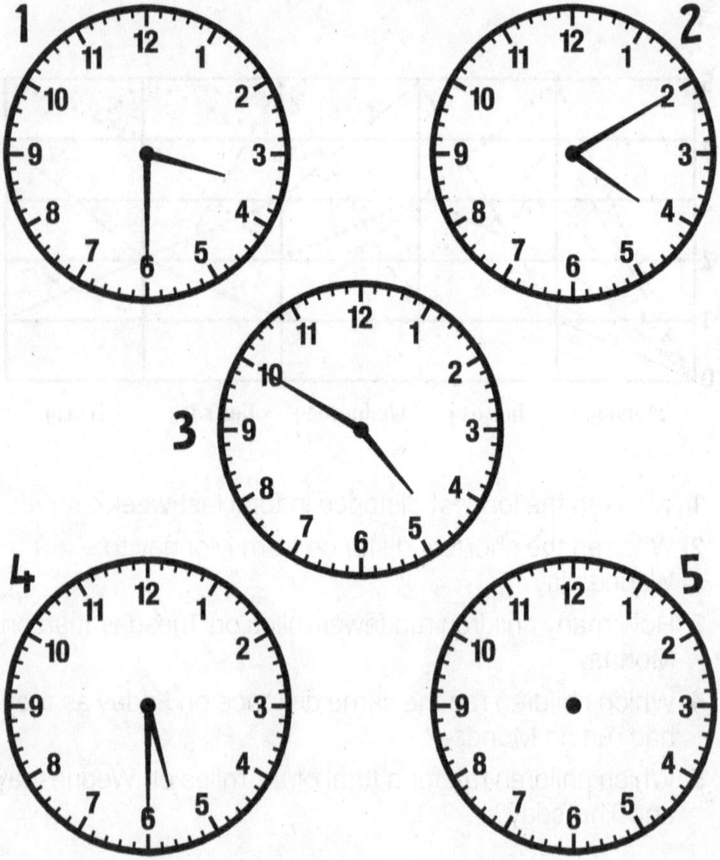

1

2

3

4

5

All in Order

Starting at 1 and finishing at 49, track your way from one square to another, either horizontally, vertically, or diagonally, placing consecutive numbers into the empty squares as you go. Some numbers are already given.

	16		10	9		32
14			8	7		30
18			5			
19			4	28	27	
21			1			36
	48	46	25		40	
49				42		

What Next?

What number is missing from each sequence? Write in the answers on each line.

A 4, 7, 9, 12, 14, 17, 19, 22, ____

B 132, 120, ____, 96, 84, 72

C 6, 7, 13, 20, 33, 53, 86, ____

D 1, 3, 6, 10, 15, 21, ____, 36, 45

E 3, 6, 12, 24, 48, ____, 192, 384

F 19, 25, 33, 43, ____, 69, 85

Abacus Additions

An abacus is a basic calculator used by sliding beads along rods to perform mathematical functions. In this puzzle, there is a simple abacus, with the 1s on the bottom rod, the 10s on the second rod, and the 100s on the third rod, but they can be much larger, often with ten rods!

At the beginning of each equation, all of the beads are on the right, and as numbers are added, they are moved to the left. Every time 10 beads reach the left, they are all moved to the right again, and one bead from the next rod up is moved to the left, as in this example of an equation, showing 46 plus 77.

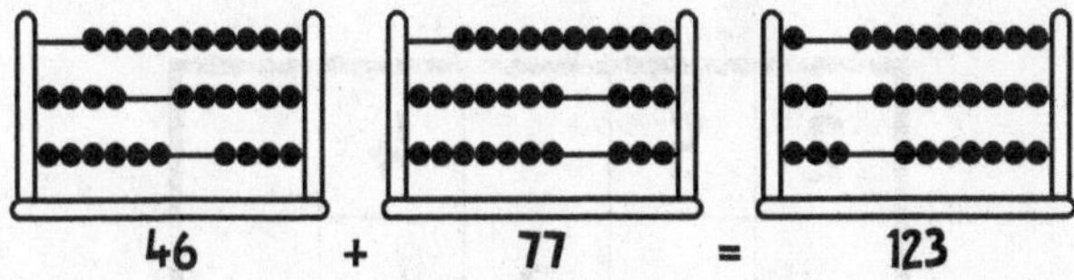

Now you can draw in the beads to show the totals after solving these equations:

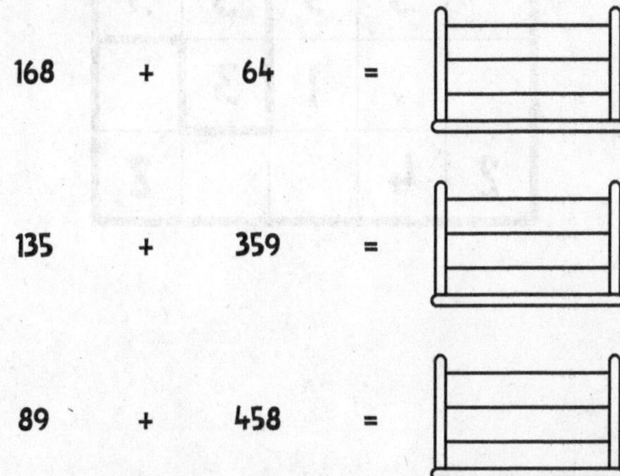

Number Grid

If you look at this grid, you'll see a group of three connected squares. Those squares are marked 3, because that's the total number of squares in the group. Draw heavy lines around other squares in the grid, so that they follow the rule, adding numbers in each empty square. For example, a square containing the number 5 must belong to a group of five squares, each filled with a 5.

2	5		4	
		2	4	
	5	5	3	3
		1	3	
2	4			2

Dominoes

A standard set of 28 dominoes has been laid out as shown. Can you draw in the edges of them all? The checkbox is provided so that you can mark them off as you find them. Dominoes can be placed either way around, 4–0 as well as 0–4. Some dominoes are already placed to help.

				5	3				
			5	0	3	0			
			1	5	4	2			
	1	4	4	4	4	3	2	5	
4	1	6	0	3	0	5	2	3	6
6	1	4	0	1	1	6	6	2	1
	2	1	2	2	6	3	6	3	
			4	5	5	0			
			6	3	5	2			
				0	0				

0-0	0-1	0-2	0-3	0-4	0-5	0-6	1-1
						✓	

1-2	1-3	1-4	1-5	1-6	2-2	2-3	2-4	2-5	2-6
									✓

3-3	3-4	3-5	3-6	4-4	4-5	4-6	5-5	5-6	6-6
				✓					

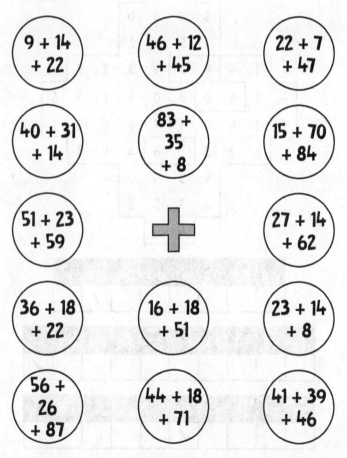

Matching Additions

Draw a line between the pairs of circles that have totals that lead to the same answer.

9 + 14 + 22

46 + 12 + 45

22 + 7 + 47

40 + 31 + 14

83 + 35 + 8

15 + 70 + 84

51 + 23 + 59

27 + 14 + 62

36 + 18 + 22

16 + 18 + 51

23 + 14 + 8

56 + 26 + 87

44 + 18 + 71

41 + 39 + 46

Switch Off

Shade some squares in this grid to switch them off, so that no number appears more than once in any row or column. No shaded square may share a side with another shaded square. When the puzzle is complete, you will be able to move from one white square to any other white square in any direction except diagonally. The first row has been done for you.

6	1	4	5	6	5
1	3	5	6	2	2
4	6	4	4	5	1
6	3	1	5	2	3
4	5	4	2	6	6
1	2	6	1	3	2

Number Workout

Write the four circled numbers in the grid to make the calculations from left to right, and from top to bottom, correct.

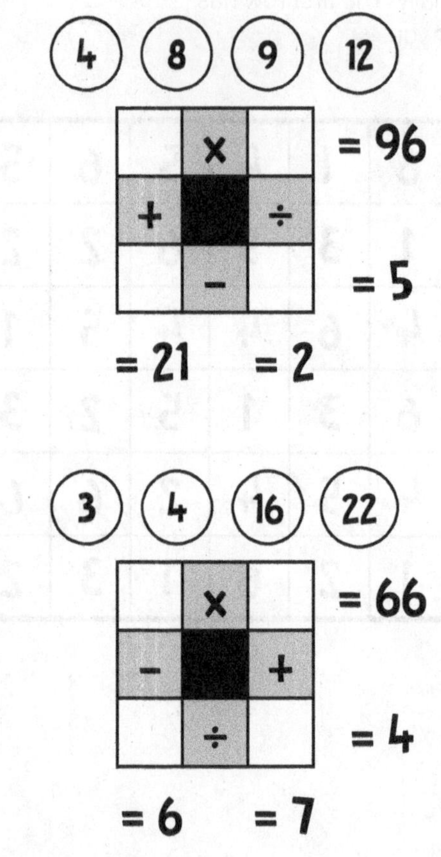

Five to One

Fill in this grid, so that each row and column contains the numbers 1 to 5 plus a single black square. Two black squares have already been filled in. The numbers along the sides of the grid indicate the first number you will encounter if you enter the grid from that direction.

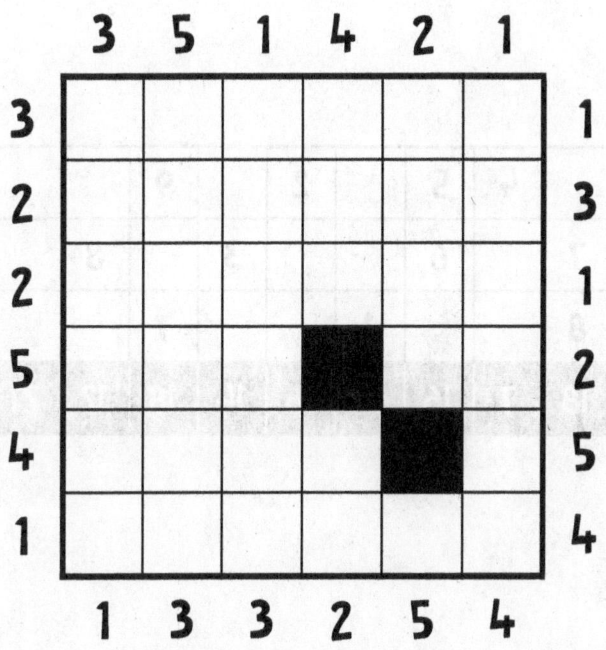

One to Nine

Fill in the empty squares, so that each row contains all the numbers from 1 to 9. Numbers can be repeated in the columns, but where one square touches another horizontally, vertically, or diagonally, the numbers must be different. The black squares show the totals when the numbers in the squares above are added together.

	4	5		2		9		
7		6			3		8	
8			1			7		
18	7	16	13	16	14	18	12	21

Square Sets

Fill each heavily outlined set of squares with different numbers from 1 to however many squares are in that set. Identical numbers that appear in the same row or column must be in squares that do not touch at the sides.

		3		2	5	4
			2		1	
	3	2		4	3	
4	5		3		4	
		3				5
2	1		4			3
3			5	3	1	

Dotted

Fill each empty square with a number from 1 to 7, so that no number appears twice in any row or column. Wherever there is a difference of just one between the numbers, there is a dot between the squares, like this:

4	3
5	2

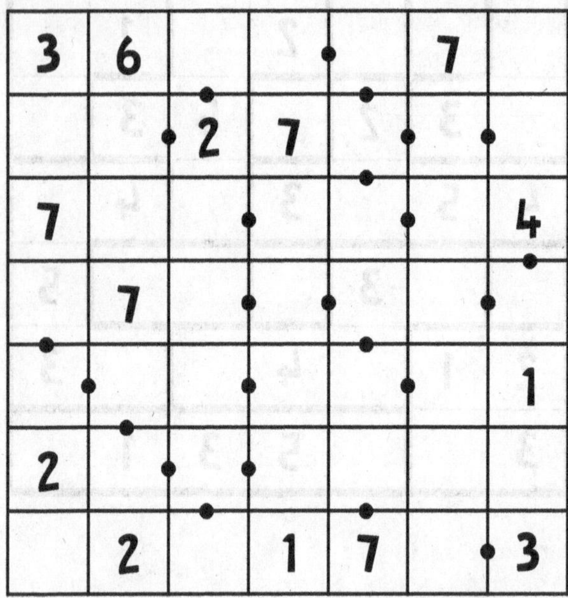

Number Link

Travel from circle to circle in any direction along the lines to find the sequence 1-2-3-4-5-6, which appears once only.

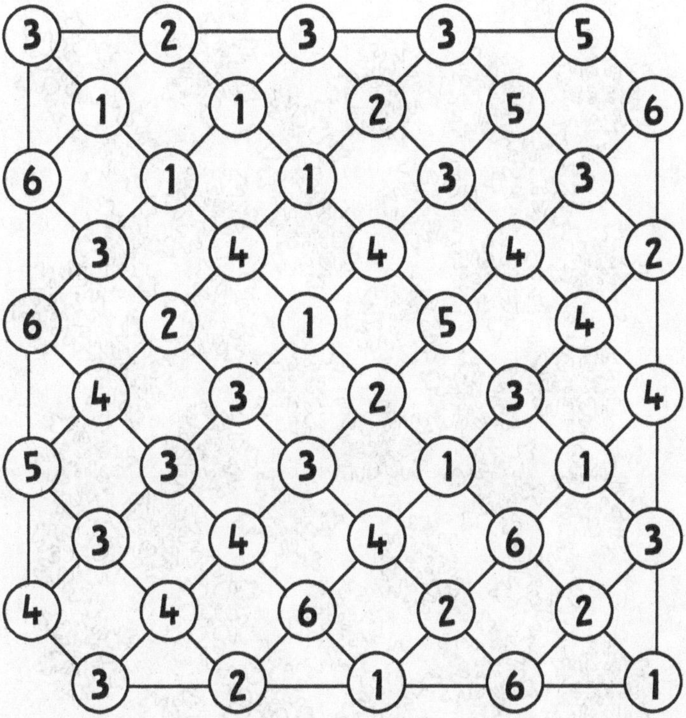

3 2 3 3 5
1 1 2 5 6
6 1 1 3 3
3 4 4 4 2
6 2 1 5 4
4 3 2 3 4
5 3 3 1 1
3 4 4 6 3
4 4 6 2 2
3 2 1 6 1

Snow Is Falling

How many snowflakes falling on this page can you count? How many whole numbers divide exactly into that number?

Train Tracking

A train made a journey from Start City to Hometown, stopping at several stations on the way. At those stations, some people got off the train, and others got on the train. Twenty people got on the train at Start City, and any passengers on the train when it reached Hometown had to get off, because that is the end of the line. How many got off at Hometown?

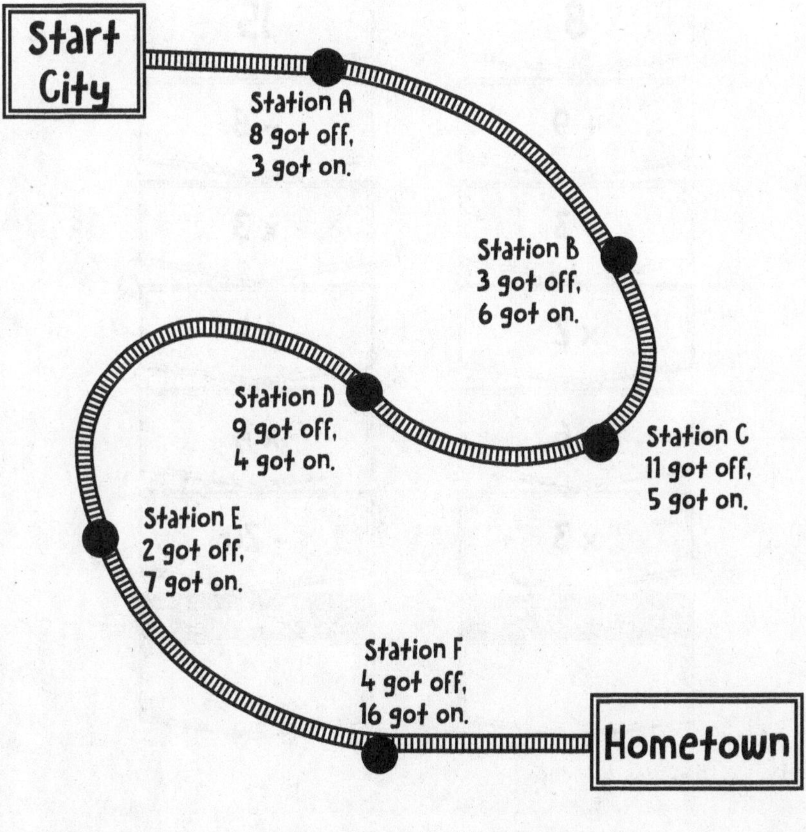

Start City

Station A
8 got off,
3 got on.

Station B
3 got off,
6 got on.

Station C
11 got off,
5 got on.

Station D
9 got off,
4 got on.

Station E
2 got off,
7 got on.

Station F
4 got off,
16 got on.

Hometown

Calculation Columns

Move down each column from top to bottom, solving the calculations as you go.

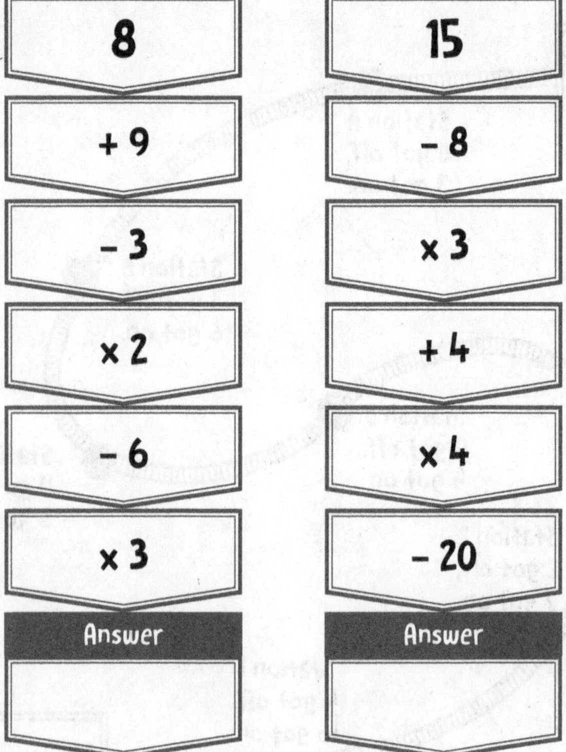

Patchwork

Every square should be filled with a number from 1 to 4, and each heavily outlined set of four squares should contain four different numbers. Every row and column must contain two of each number.

When two squares share a side shown by thick lines, the numbers in them must be different.

		4		2		4	
3			1			3	2
2			2	3	4	1	
		2	1	4		2	1
		3					
3	4				1		2
	2						4
4				1	4		

Remainders

No number divides exactly into 37; there is always a number left over (a remainder). Solve these equations, then write the remainder in the box, as shown in the first equation. When you have finished, add up all of the remainder numbers. What is the answer?

3 | 37 = 12 r = 1

2 | 37 r =

4 | 37 r =

5 | 37 r =

8 | 37 r =

7 | 37 r =

6 | 37 r =

Route 66

Fill in the empty squares, so that the numbers in every row, column, and diagonal line of five squares add up to 66.

21	19	8		
9	7	22		9
			20	15
12			13	
9	21	10		15

Better Balance

Compare the items on the scales to find out what each shape weighs. Two weights are already given. Which shape can you add to the left side of the bottom scale to make both sides level?

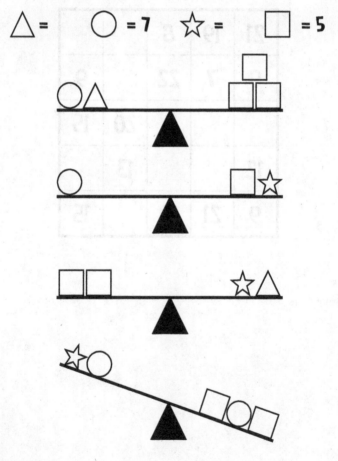

△ = ○ = 7 ☆ = □ = 5

Fractions

What fraction of each of these squares has been shaded black?

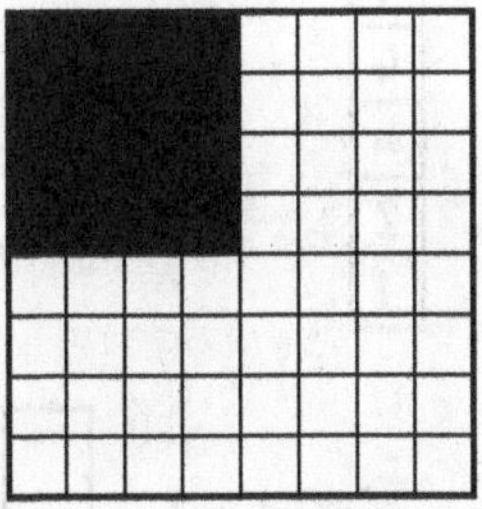

A

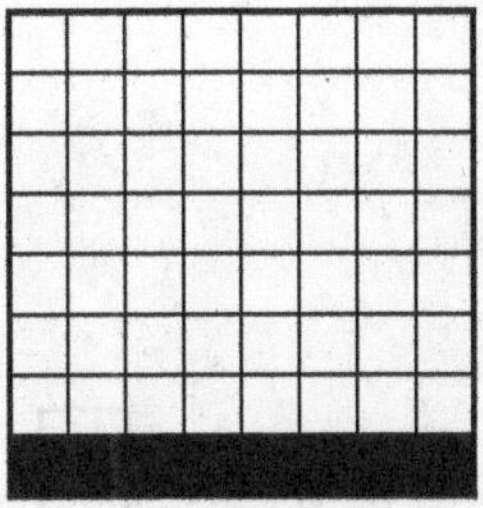

B

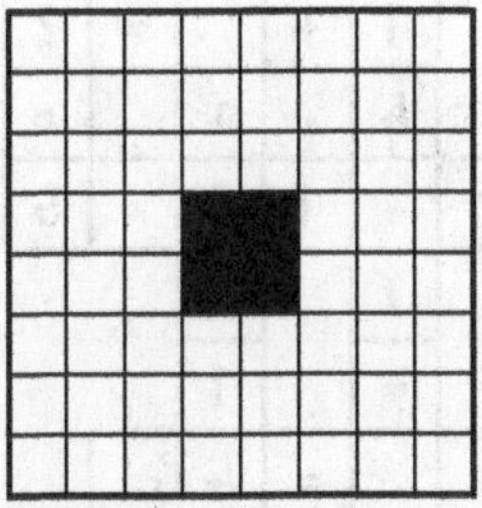

C

D

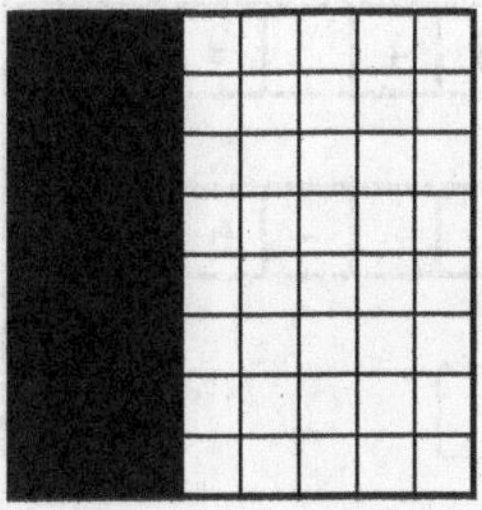

E

F

Crisscross Equations

Fill in the missing numbers, one digit per square, so that the equations are correct. Numbers that have two digits will appear in two boxes, reading either left to right or top to bottom, like this:

16 + 9 = 25

7 + 14 = 21

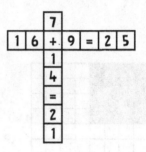

Chains

Write the numbers 1 to 5 in the empty circles below, so that the numbers appear just once in every row, column, and connected set of five circles.

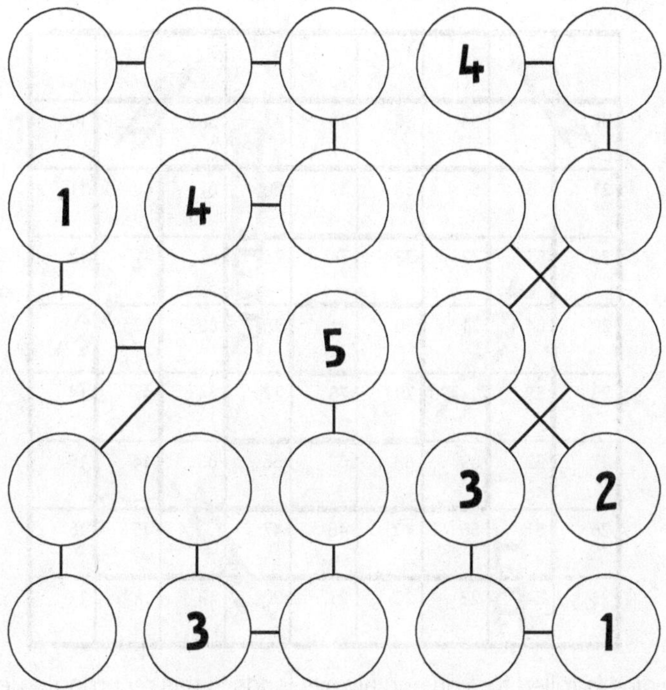

Ladders and Ladders

In this version of the popular game chutes and ladders, work in a clockwise direction from the top left corner of the board toward the middle. When you throw a number and land at the top or the bottom of a ladder, you climb or descend it to the end (sometimes to a higher number and sometimes to a lower number), then continue from that square.

1	2	3	4	5	6	7	8	9
32	33	34	35	36	37	38	39	10
31	56	57	58	59	60	61	40	11
30	55	72	73	74	75	62	41	12
29	54	71	80	81	76	63	42	13
28	53	70	79	78	77	64	43	14
27	52	69	68	67	66	65	44	15
26	51	50	49	48	47	46	45	16
25	24	23	22	21	20	19	18	17

The dice is rolled for you and always lands in this recurring order: 5, 2, 1, 4, 3, 6. Start by placing your counter on square 5. You need an exact number to finish the game on the middle square—counting backward if you don't end on square 81. For example, if you land on square 79 and throw a six, you will have to go back to square 77.

Borders

Divide this grid into rectangles, each containing a single number. The number in each rectangle must match the number of squares enclosed by it. One has already been done for you.

		3		6	
	6		2		
2		4			
	3			1	5
	4			6	

Hexagony

Can you place the hexagons into the grid, so that where any hexagon touches another along a straight line, the number in both triangles is the same? No rotation of any hexagon is allowed! One number is already in place.

6
1 0
3 5
7

2
0 8
3 5
9

7
2 4
1 0
8

2

7
3 6
0 9
1

1
5 3
4 6
2

7
6 4
8 2
3

2
9 8
3 6
7

Pathfinder

Draw a single path from the top left square to the bottom right square of the grid, moving through all of the squares in either a horizontal, vertical, or diagonal direction. Lines should only pass through a square once, and your path should take you through the numbers in the sequence 1-2-3-4-5-6-1-2-3-4-5-6, etc. Some parts of the path are already in place. Can you find the way through?

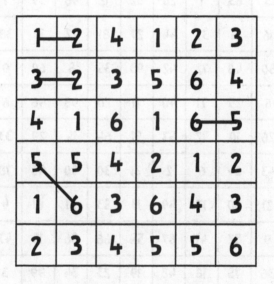

1	2	4	1	2	3
3	2	3	5	6	4
4	1	6	1	6	5
5	5	4	2	1	2
1	6	3	6	4	3
2	3	4	5	5	6

Three by Three

Draw a path through the grid from the top arrow to the bottom arrow, moving up, down, and across, but not diagonally. You must cross every number that is divisible by three, and any may appear more than once on your way through.

3	63	1	28	52	12	96	39	7
16	15	37	44	27	81	22	51	38
50	48	72	42	93	35	5	69	9
8	25	71	40	11	20	98	46	6
26	10	72	57	51	64	14	29	33
43	84	6	2	21	30	90	45	78
21	60	17	49	13	53	31	61	4
9	32	41	87	54	66	36	15	47
36	75	18	48	19	23	34	99	3

Coin Collecting

Can you find the 18 hidden coins? One is already in place. Squares with numbers do not contain coins, but where a number appears in a square, it indicates how many coins are located in the squares surrounding it and touching it at any corner or side. Draw in the missing coins. You may find it helps if you place a small cross in any square that does not contain a coin.

2	2			2	2		1
		2			2	2	
2	3	2		1	1		
				1			1
		2				3	
	3		2	2			
2		3	4			3	
	2			2	2	●	1

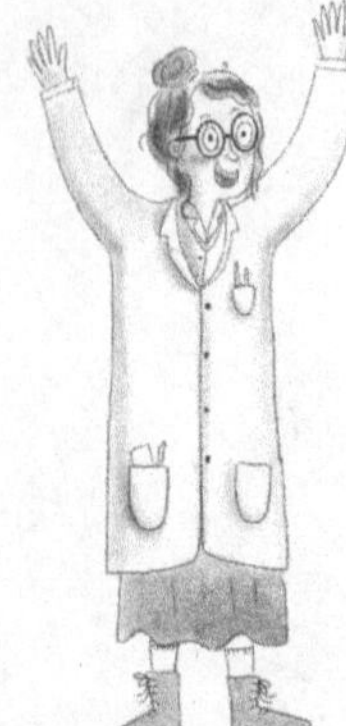

Calculation Chain

Solve the first equation, then copy your answer into the box indicated by the arrow. Then solve that equation, and do the same again until you reach a final answer in the shaded box.

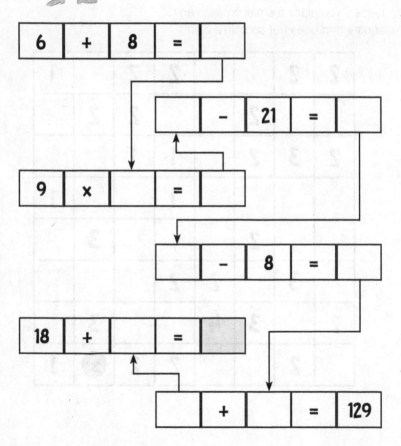

6	+	8	=	

	–	21	=	

9	x		=	

	–	8	=	

18	+		=	

	+		=	129

Cross-referencing

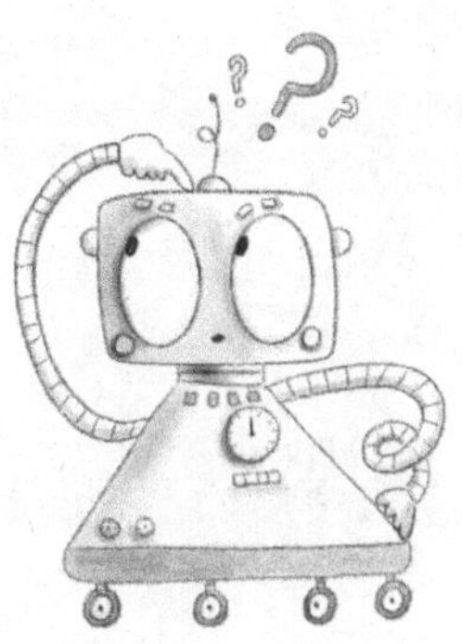

Cross-reference the numbers in the horizontal rows and vertical columns of the grid below, and calculate the totals when the two numbers are multiplied together.

One has already been done as an example: 8 x 11 = 88.

	7	3	11	9	4	5
2						
12						
8			88			
10						
6						
7						

Addition Deletions

Delete two of the three numbers in every box in order to make these addition equations work.

22 11 9	+	34 17 6	=	39
9 37 45	+	20 26 43	=	52
19 5 4	+	18 1 10	=	23
42 16 41	+	24 32 47	=	73
36 32 15	+	23 4 31	=	46
25 14 38	+	49 3 18	=	74

Equation Circles

Starting at the top, place one number in every empty circle to make the total correct, then continue down to the next equation that those numbers produce.

		5	4	9
−		3	7	2
		◯	◯	◯
+		1	3	5
		◯	◯	◯
×				8
	◯	◯	◯	◯

Square Sets

Fill each heavily outlined set of squares with different numbers from 1 to however many squares are in that set. Identical numbers that appear in the same row or column must be in squares that do not touch at the sides.

			3		1	5
3		2	1			
1	3				3	
		4	2	5		2
4			3			4
	2		1		4	
3		1				2

Spotted and Dotted

Fill each empty square with a number from 1 to 7, so that no number appears twice in any row or column. Wherever there is a difference of just one between the numbers, there is a dot between the squares, like this:

4 • 3
5 2

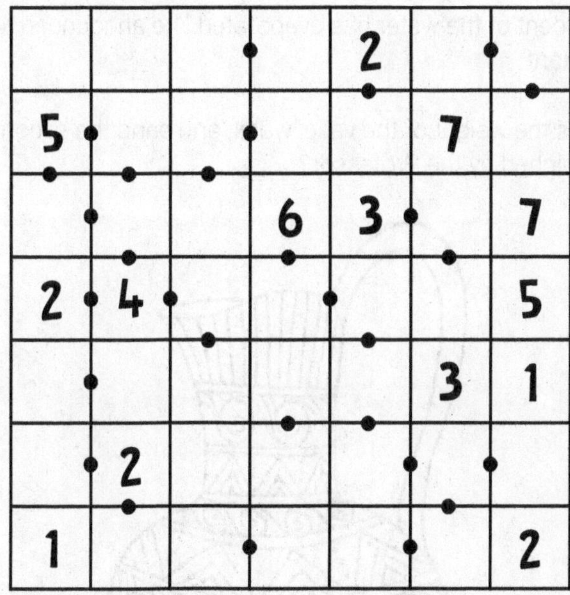

The Professor's Puzzle

The Professor was conducting an experiment. He put a vase weighing four units on his scale. Then he weighed 24 units of water and added one unit of sand. The total weight of the vase, water, and sand amounted to 29 units.

The Professor then placed it on a windowsill in the sunshine. A few days later, he weighed the vase and its contents again.

"Fifty percent of the water has evaporated," he announced to his assistant.

What was the weight of the vase, water, and sand the second time it was weighed by the Professor?

Flower Fest

Each of these flowers represents a different number: 2, 4, 5, or 7. Figure out the value of each of the four different flowers to make the totals correct.

−

2 2

+

7 8

+

9 9

−

2 3

Shapes and Numbers

Count the sides on each shape. Can you figure out which number is equal to C? Write the number on the line.

= 369

A

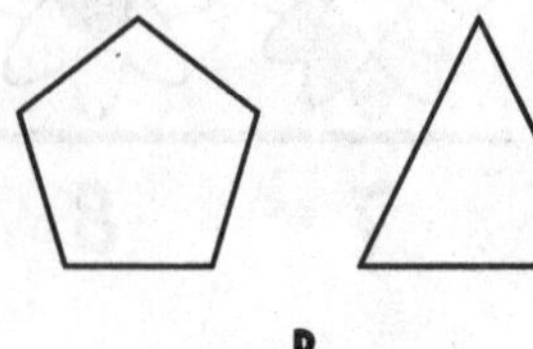

= 538

B

= ______

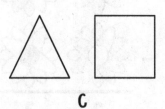

C

Multiplication Deletions

Delete two of the three numbers in every box, in order to make these multiplication equations work.

7 8 9	×	8 7 6	=	72
12 16 11	×	4 7 6	=	64
6 7 8	×	13 14 15	=	84
17 13 21	×	7 5 4	=	91
16 12 14	×	14 13 9	=	126
8 4 6	×	19 17 13	=	136

What's Missing?

Place a different number from 1 to 9 into each empty square, so that every horizontal row and every vertical column adds up to the numbers at the end of that row or column. Two numbers are already in place, so be sure not to use them again.

8	+		+		=	23
+		+		+		
	+		+		=	13
+		+		+		
	+		+	4	=	9
=		=		=		
17		10		18		

Sudoku

Fill the empty squares in the grid, so that there is one of every number in each row, column, and mini-grid of nine squares. Use single-digit numbers from 1 to 9.

8		1	6				9	4
		6	2	8		1		3
		7				6		5
7	2		4	9			3	
4			8	3	2			7
	9			7	1		2	8
3		9				7		
5		4		2	3	8		
1	8				5	3		9

Switch Off

Shade some squares in this grid to switch them off, so that no number appears more than once in any row or column. No shaded square may share a side with another shaded square. When the puzzle is complete, you will be able to move from one white square to any other white square in any direction except diagonally. The first row has been done for you.

1	1	3	1	7	2	6
2	4	1	3	6	1	4
5	6	4	1	4	3	1
7	4	6	7	6	1	5
1	2	4	1	5	7	4
7	1	2	4	7	6	1
5	3	5	3	1	4	5

Shape Up

Subtract a number in each star from a number in a square to equal a number in a circle. Each shape is only used once. Draw lines to link each of the three shapes together.

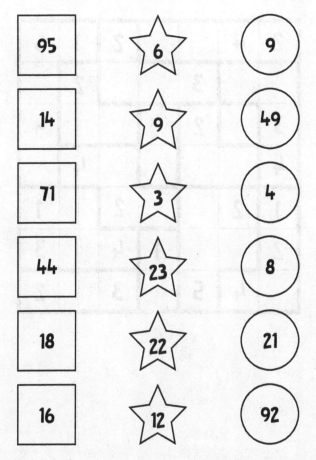

Squares	Stars	Circles
95	6	9
14	9	49
71	3	4
44	23	8
18	22	21
16	12	92

Square Sets

Fill each heavily outlined set of squares with different numbers from 1 to however many squares are in that set. Identical numbers that appear in the same row or column must be in squares that do not touch at the sides.

2	4			2	1	5
		3			2	
3		2				4
4					4	
1	2			2		1
2			1	4		3
	4	5		3		2

Square Numbers

What number is missing in this series of squares?

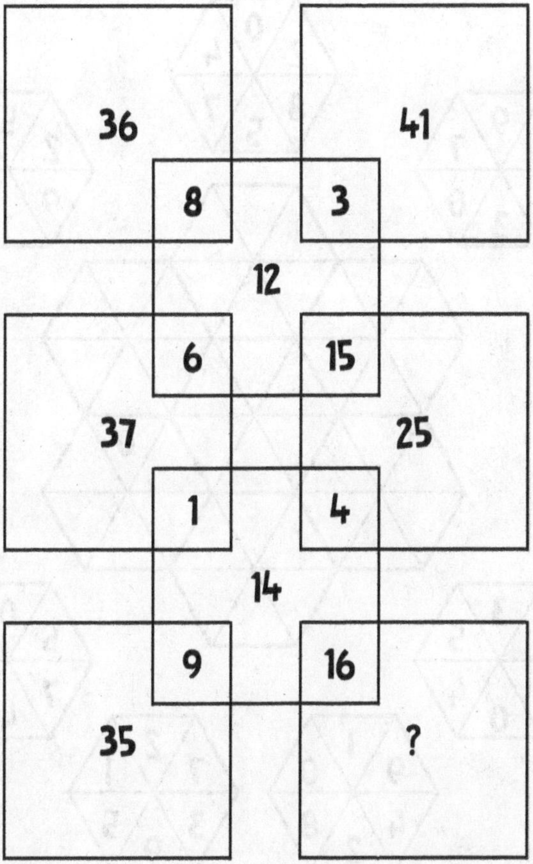

36		41
8		3
	12	
6		15
37		25
1		4
	14	
9		16
35		?

Hexagony

Can you place the hexagons into the grid, so that where any hexagon touches another along a straight line, the number in both triangles is the same? No rotation of any hexagon is allowed. One number is already in place.

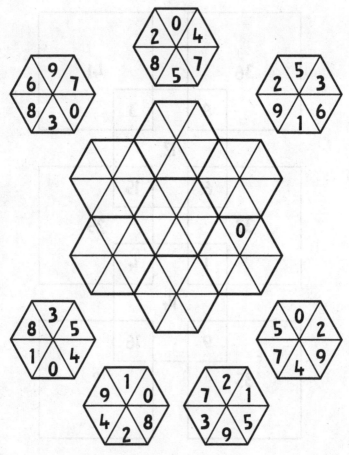

Mathological

Fill each empty square with a number from 1 to 5. No number may appear twice in any row or column. Circles on the grid give clues to the numbers in the four squares that they touch. If a circle contains a number and an addition sign (+), then that is the total of the numbers in diagonally adjacent cells. For example, "7+" means that when the numbers in two diagonally adjacent squares are added together, the answer is "7."

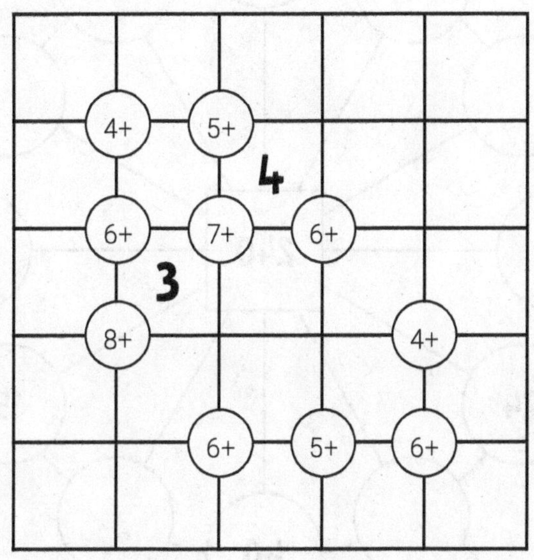

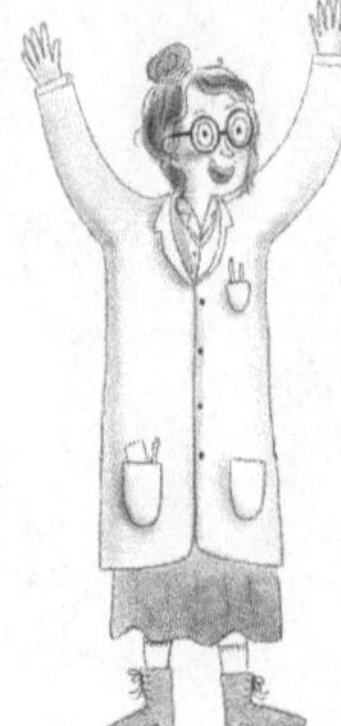

Number-Go-Round

Place the given numbers in the empty circles, so that—when multiplied by the number diagonally or directly opposite—they equal the number in the square in the middle.

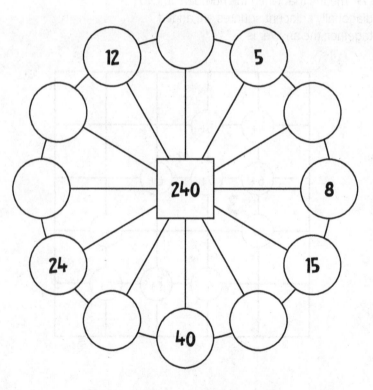

6 10 16 20 30 48

Candle Countdown

Standard candles (A) burn at the rate of 1 inch per hour, wide candles (B) burn at the rate of 1/2 inch per hour, and narrow candles (C) burn at the rate of 2 inches per hour. The candles depicted below are all 6 inches high. To make them all finish burning at exactly eight o'clock tonight, at what time should each one be lit?

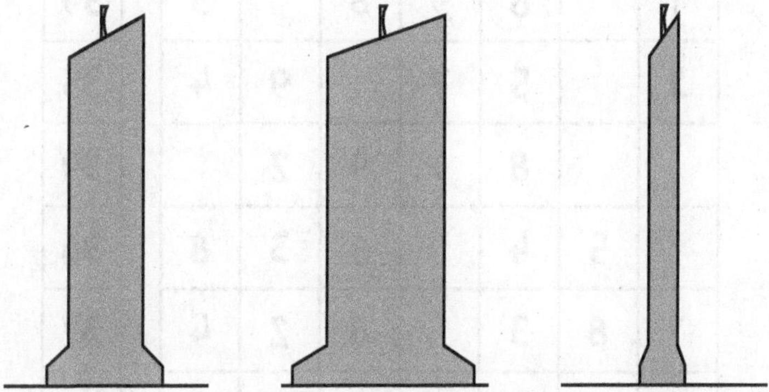

A B C

Total Concentration

Can you fill in the missing numbers so that each row, each column, and two diagonal lines of seven squares add up to the totals given at the end of each row, column, and diagonal line? Use numbers from 1 to 9 only.

							37
1		6	9	8		3	39
3		5	7		9	4	35
		8	1	9	2		39
	5	4		6	3	8	36
7	8	3		8	2	4	37
9	1				8	6	38
3	7	5	7	6		2	33
30	35	40	42	43	34	33	38

Mathematics Crossword

Solve the equations, then enter the answers into the grid, one digit per square.

1		2	■	3		4
	■	5			■	
6	7		■	8	9	
■		■	■	■		■
10		11	■	12		13
	■	14			■	
15			■	16		

Across

1 111 x 5
3 9 x 12
5 123 + 123
6 12 x 12
8 80 + 85
10 64 + 40
12 149 – 16
14 190 + 31
15 300 x 3
16 220 x 4

Down

1 560 – 19
2 300 + 224
3 80 + 81
4 821 – 16
7 20 x 20
9 700 – 57
10 120 – 11
11 360 + 60
12 126 – 8
13 150 + 150

Six Square

Place a number from 1 to 6 in each empty square, so that when the numbers in each heavily outlined shape are added together, they equal the small number in the top left corner. No number may appear twice in any horizontal row or vertical column of five squares. One set and some extra numbers have already been entered to start you off.

15	7 **4**	4		11 **6**	
	2	10			
	1	13	14	9	
16		**2**		**5**	5
				8	
4		10	**6**		

Cross Numbers

Fit nine different numbers from 1 to 9 into every empty square to make the calculations correct. Two of the nine numbers are already in place, so be sure not to use them again.

	×		×	6	=	126
×	■	×	■	×		
	×		×		=	80
×	■	×	■	×		
	×	1	×		=	36
=		=		=		
126		15		192		

Six in Place

Every row and column of this grid should contain one each of the numbers 1, 2, 3, 4, 5, and 6.
In addition, each of the six shapes (marked by thicker lines) should also contain one each of the numbers 1, 2, 3, 4, 5, and 6. Can you complete the grid?

4		2		3	
5		1		6	
	2				
2	6				
			4		
1	3				

Crafty Kakuro

Place one of the numbers on either side of the grid in each empty square, so that the numbers in each row total the number in the black square to the left, and the numbers in each column total the number in the black square above it. The numbers you use in every set, either across or down, must be different.

Some numbers are already in place, and these are crossed off the list. Cross out the rest as you use them, so you don't lose track.

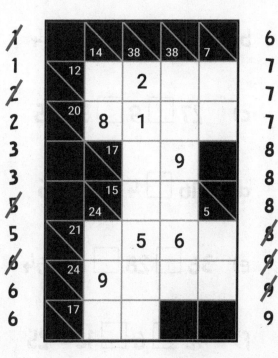

~~1~~	■	14	38	38	7	6
1	12		2			7
~~2~~	20	8	1			7
2	■	17		9	■	7
3	■	15 / 24			5	8
3	21		5	6		8
~~5~~	24	9				8
5	17			■	■	~~8~~
~~6~~						~~9~~
6						~~9~~
6						9

Signs

Fill each empty square with a mathematical sign (+, −, x, or ÷) to make each answer correct. Use two different signs in every line, and solve the equations as they appear in order from left to right.

a) 15 ☐ 2 ☐ 13 = 43

b) 51 ☐ 23 ☐ 2 = 14

c) 27 ☐ 9 ☐ 5 = 15

d) 16 ☐ 4 ☐ 4 = 5

e) 36 ☐ 28 ☐ 8 = 64

f) 42 ☐ 6 ☐ 18 = 25

Hexaddition

Fit six different numbers from 1 to 9 into the six hexagons that surround each black hexagon. The numbers in all six white hexagons should add up to the number in the black one. Some are already in place.

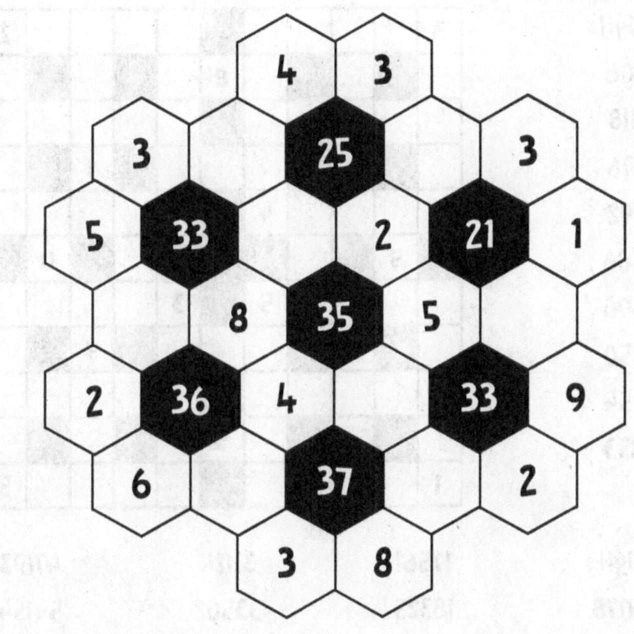

Two Too Many

The grid can be filled with all of the listed numbers, except for two. Which two will not fit?

Some digits are already in place to get you started.

3					■					2
	■		■		8		■		■	
					■					
	■	6	■				■	1	■	
				4	■	4				
■	9	■		■	■	■		■	0	■
				5	■	3				
	■	2	■				■	9	■	
					■					
	■		■		5		■		■	
1					■					5

3 digits

106
118
176
192
486
596
750
754
853

5 digits

12078
13216
13802
14102
15567
16264
17561
18325
21785
22255
24075
26563
29060
31124
33502
34262
37125
41714
42185
45621
47613
54154
57097
58172
63001

Missing Number

Which number is missing in this sequence?

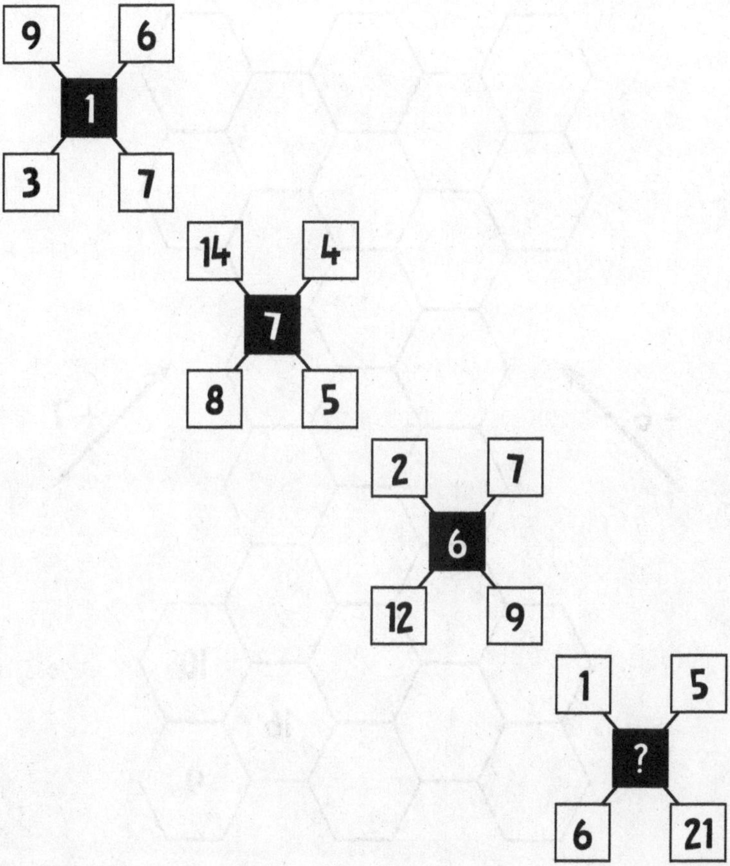

9		6
	1	
3		7

14		4
	7	
8		5

2		7
	6	
12		9

1		5
	?	
6		21

Hexagon Equations

Fill in the missing numbers in this pattern. Work from the bottom to the top. When moving up to the left, add seven to the previous number; and when moving up to the right, subtract six from the previous number. Three numbers are already in place.

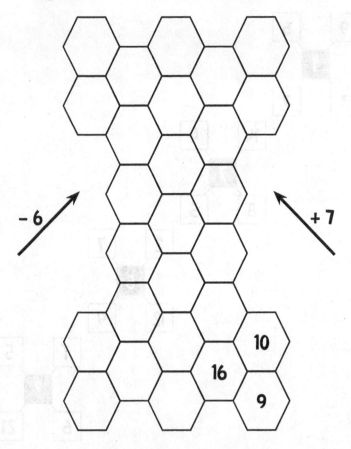

– 6

+ 7

10

16

9

Calculation Chain

Solve the first equation, then copy your answer into the box indicated by the arrow. Then solve that equaltion, and do the same again until you reach the final answer in the shaded box.

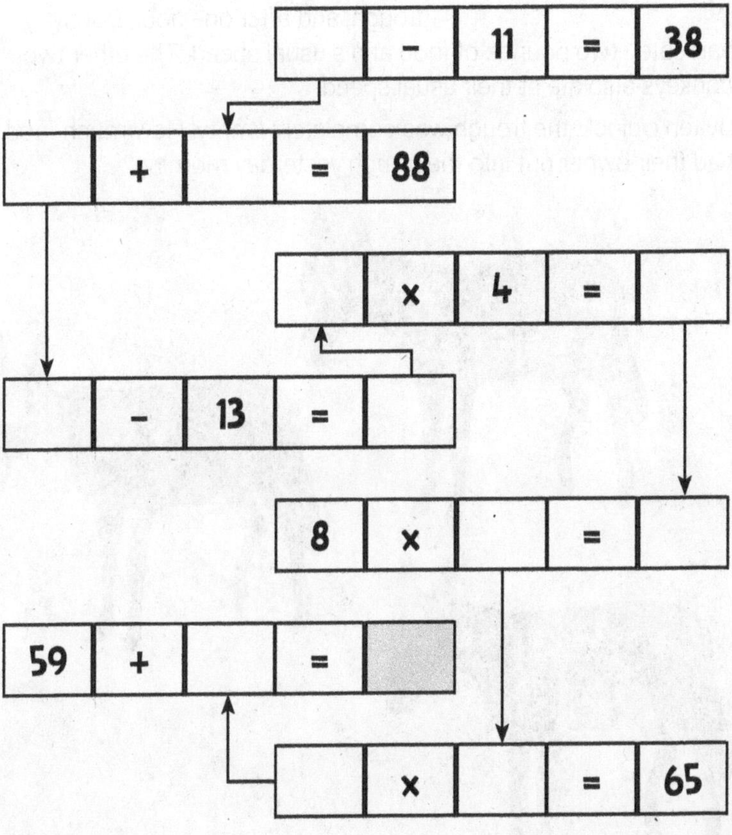

	−	11	=	38

	+		=	88

	×	4	=	

	−	13	=	

8	×		=	

59	+		=	

	×		=	65

Donkeys' Diets

Danny, Denny, and Donny are three donkeys who like their food!

Danny eats twice as fast as Denny, and Denny eats twice as fast as Donny.

At nine o'clock yesterday morning, their owner put out the food in the stable, filling the trough almost to the top.

All of the donkeys ate from the same trough, and after one hour, Donny had eaten two pounds of food at his usual speed. The other two donkeys also ate at their usual speed.

By ten o'clock, the trough was completely empty. How much food had their owner put into the trough yesterday morning?

More Donkeys

Danny, Denny, and Donny have been joined by two new baby donkeys, who also like their food!

Dilly eats half as fast as Doris, who eats half as fast as Donny.

At nine o'clock this morning, their owner put out the food in the stable—this time filling the trough to the very top, since extra food was needed for the new arrivals, and all five donkeys ate at their usual speed.

By ten o'clock, the trough was completely empty. How much more food did their owner need to put into the trough this morning for this to be possible?

What's It Worth?

Each of these different shapes can be replaced by a number. Can you find out what each shape is worth to make the equations work? Solve the equations in the order in which they appear, working from left to right or from top to bottom.

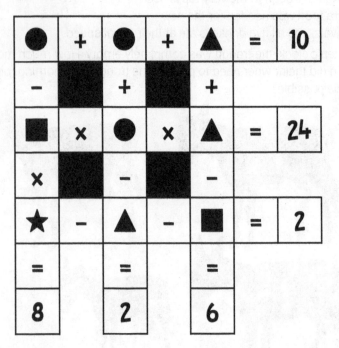

●	+	●	+	▲	=	10
−		+		+		
■	×	●	×	▲	=	24
×		−		−		
★	−	▲	−	■	=	2
=		=		=		
8		2		6		

Birds on a Wire

Josh is an avid birdwatcher and noticed yesterday that several birds landed on a wire. He started to watch them at ten o'clock yesterday morning and wrote down his observations. Can you do the same? Fill in the chart below, showing the times that Josh made his entries and how many birds were on the wire at that moment.

Time	Number of birds that flew off	Number of birds that landed	Total number of birds on the wire
10:00	–	–	2

At 10:00 a.m. there were two birds on the wire.

Five minutes later, one bird flew off, and four birds landed on the wire.

Four minutes later, two birds flew off, and five birds landed on the wire.

Seven minutes later, eight birds flew off, and 11 birds landed on the wire.

Six minutes later, ten birds flew off, and four birds landed on the wire.

Five minutes later, three birds flew off, and 12 birds landed on the wire.

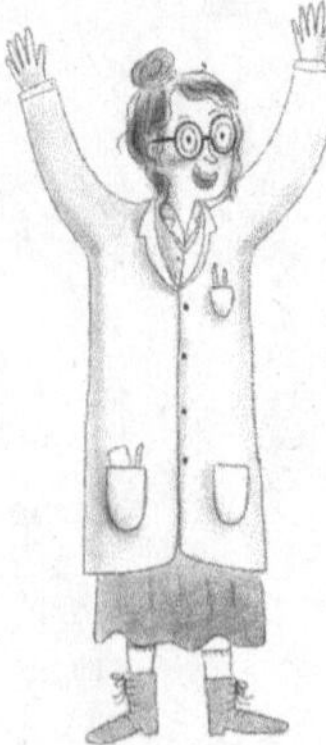

Mathematics Crossword

Solve the equations, then enter the answers in the grid, one digit per square.

1		■	2	■	3	
	■	■	4	5		■
	■	6			■	■
7			■	8		9
■	■	10	11		■	
■	12			■	■	
13		■		■	14	

Across

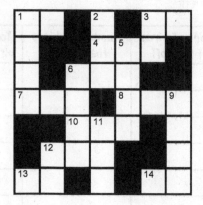

1 12 Down x 3
3 Days in six weeks
4 10 Across – 146
6 10 Across + 74
7 178 x 3
8 120 – 11
10 115 x 4
12 4 Across – 92
13 14 Across – 2
14 8 x 8

Down

1 9 Down ÷ 6 Down
2 7 Across + 197
3 3 Across – 1
5 1,882 x 5
6 4,000 – 551
9 5 Down + 134
11 2 Down – 32
12 11 + 11

Long-distance Runners

Three friends took part in a race. They ran around the track four times. Can you fill in the chart to show the time each took to run the first, second, third, and fourth laps of the course? Then you can add up all of their times to discover who won the race!

Runner	Lap 1	Lap 2	Lap 3	Lap 4	Total Time (seconds)
Georgie					
Hal					
Indira					

Georgie ran lap 1 in 58 seconds, lap 2 in 56 seconds, and lap 3 in 59 seconds.

Hal ran lap 1 in 57 seconds, lap 2 in 60 seconds, and lap 3 in 55 seconds.

Indira ran lap 1 in 56 seconds, lap 2 in 54 seconds, and lap 3 in 61 seconds.

In lap 4, Georgie finished two seconds slower than Indira, and Indiara finished one second faster than Hal, who finished lap 4 in 63 seconds.

Equation Square

All the digits from 1 to 9 are used in this grid, but only once each. Can you figure out their positions in the grid to make the equations work?

Solve the equations in the order in which they appear, working from left to right or from top to bottom. Two of the numbers are already in place, so be sure not to use them again.

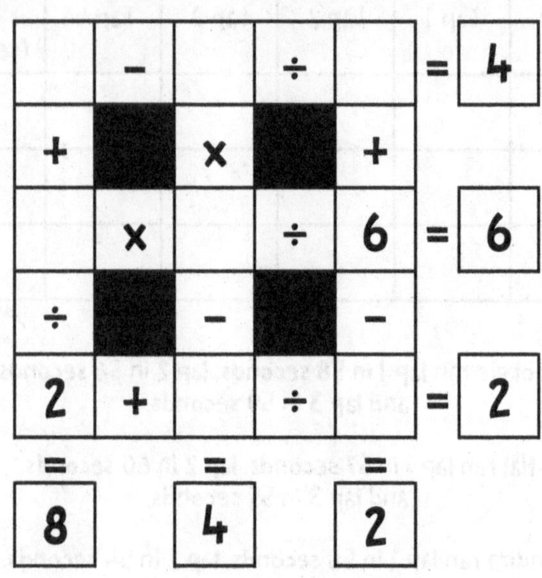

★★★

Crossing Out

Cross out two of the three numbers in every box in order to make these equations work.

12 13 14	+	16 22 26	=	34
67 65 63	÷	9 7 8	=	9
47 43 49	–	17 21 19	=	24
36 38 44	+	15 19 17	=	63
8 9 4	×	6 12 7	=	56
88 84 72	÷	7 6 8	=	14

Five Square

Place a number from 1 to 5 in each empty square, so that when the numbers in each heavily outlined shape are multiplied together, they equal the number in the top left corner. No number may appear twice in any horizontal row or vertical column of five squares. Two have already been entered to get you started.

15	6	20		8
5		24	5	
2		12	**3**	15
20		2		

Calculation Columns

Move down each column from top to bottom, solving each calculation as you go.

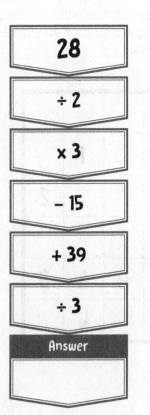

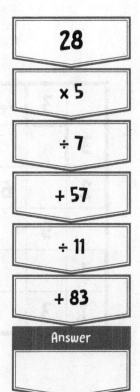

28	28
÷ 2	× 5
× 3	÷ 7
– 15	+ 57
+ 39	÷ 11
÷ 3	+ 83
Answer	Answer

Number Grid

If you look at the top row of this grid, you'll see a group of three connected squares. Those squares are marked 3, because that's the total number of squares in the group. Draw heavy lines around other squares in the grid, so that they follow the rule, adding numbers in each empty square. For example, a square containing the number 6 must belong to a group of six squares, each filled with a 6.

	3	4			
3				1	
2		6			2
	5		2		
3			6	6	3
1	3			4	

Petal Problem

The numbers on which three petals of the same shade can be multiplied together to give the highest total?

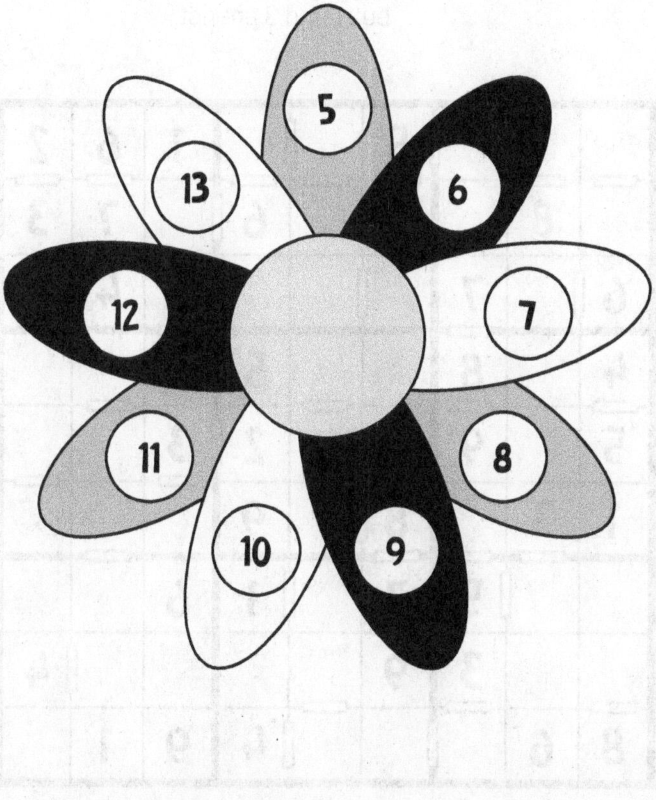

5

13

6

12

7

11

8

10

9

Consecutive Sudoku

Fill the empty squares in this grid, so that every horizontal row, vertical column, and mini grid contains different numbers from 1 to 9.
Wherever two touching squares contain consecutive numbers, there is a bar between them. Consecutive numbers have a difference of one: for example, the numbers 1 and 2 are consecutive, but 1 and 3 are not.

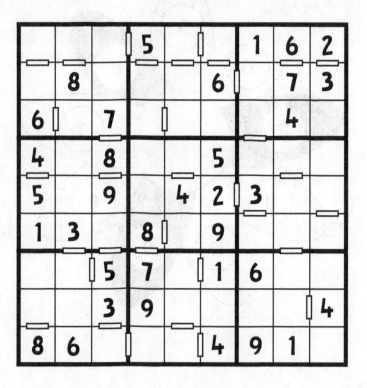

			5			1	6	2
	8				6		7	3
6		7					4	
4		8			5			
5		9		4	2	3		
1	3		8		9			
		5	7		1	6		
		3	9					4
8	6				4	9	1	

Addition Maze

Work your way through the maze from top to bottom, adding up the numbers on the way and filling in the total at the end.

There are lots of different numbers, but you should only use those that are on the correct path through the maze.

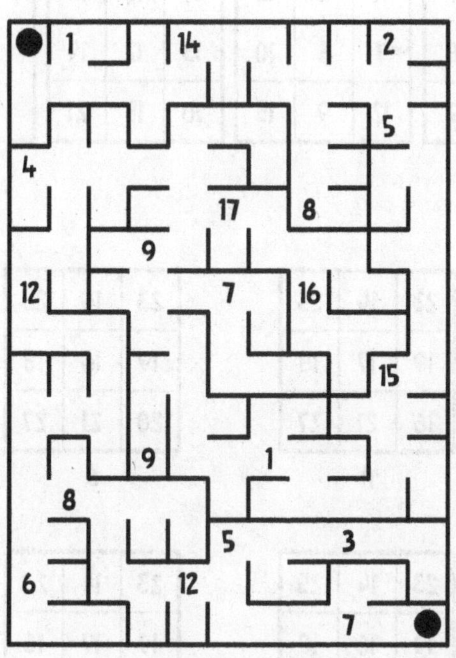

What Next?

Which of the four lettered alternatives (A, B, C, or D) fits most logically into the empty square?

5	2	7
1	4	6
8	3	9

11	6	13
7	8	10
12	9	15

17	10	19
13	12	14
16	15	21

?

23	14	25
19	17	18
16	21	27

A

23	14	23
19	16	18
20	21	27

B

23	14	25
19	16	18
20	21	27

C

23	14	23
19	17	18
16	21	27

D

★★★

Mathsearch

Solve the equations, then see if you can find the answers in the grid. The answers can run backward or forward, in either a horizontal, vertical, or diagonal direction.

8	9	2	6	1	1	4	7	4	1
8	8	0	2	0	8	5	4	4	0
3	3	2	7	8	8	9	5	5	0
4	1	5	7	2	2	6	1	4	1
4	6	1	1	5	2	7	6	1	3
2	9	3	8	9	5	8	3	0	8
2	3	2	9	1	1	2	6	2	0
2	4	8	8	4	7	9	6	1	6
3	7	3	9	7	9	4	3	9	9
5	4	7	6	0	6	0	1	9	0

232 + 989 =

678 + 876 =

1,020 – 22 =

38 x 40 =

3,776 + 3,776 =

10,010 ÷ 10 =

345 x 4 =

9,743 – 974 =

332 + 332 + 332 =

4,906 x 3 =

864 + 468 =

63,636 ÷ 6 =

Dominoes

A set of 28 dominoes has been laid out as shown. Can you draw around the edges of them all? Use the checkbox to mark them off as you find them. Dominoes can be placed either way around, 4–0 as well as 0–4. The domino already placed will help you get started.

				2	2				
			4	4	3	6			
			2	6	3	2			
	5	3	6	0	2	4	1	5	
0	2	0	3	1	6	5	6	6	2
0	4	4	1	4	6	0	4	1	5
	5	6	1	0	5	0	3	3	
			2	4	1	3			
			1	1	5	3			
				0	5				

0–0	0–1	0–2	0–3	0–4	0–5	0–6	1–1
				✓			

1–2	1–3	1–4	1–5	1–6	2–2	2–3	2–4	2–5	2–6
						✓			

3–3	3–4	3–5	3–6	4–4	4–5	4–6	5–5	5–6	6–6
									✓

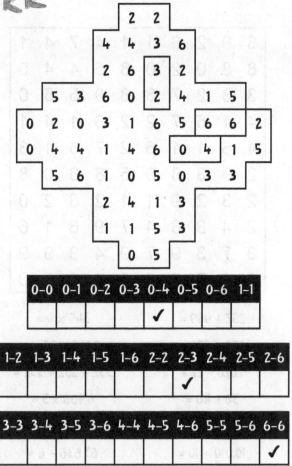

Equation Problem

Fill in each empty square with either a number or mathematical symbol (+, −, x, or ÷), so that the totals are correct in each row and column, and in each of the two shaded diagonal lines of five squares in the middle of the grid, reading from top to bottom.

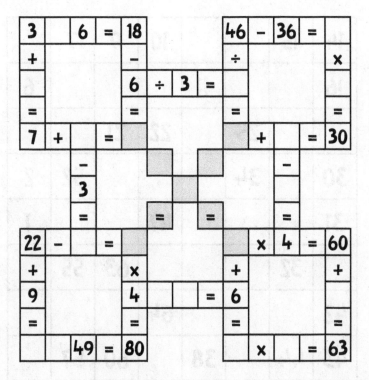

3		6	=	18				46	−	36	=	
+				−				÷				x
				6	÷	3	=					
=				=				=				=
7	+		=						+		=	30
		−								−		
		3										
		=			=		=			=		
22	−		=						x	4	=	60
+				x				+				+
9				4			=	6				
=				=				=				=
		49	=	80					x		=	63

All in Order

Starting at 1 and finishing at 64, track your way from one square to another, horizontally, vertically, or diagonally, placing consecutive numbers in the empty squares as you go. Some numbers are already given.

14	15			10	9	7	
16			11				6
		25		22	21		
30		34				52	2
31				47			1
	32				63	55	
42				64			
43	44		38		60	57	

Mathological

Fill each empty square with a number from 1 to 6. No number may appear twice in any row or column. Circles on the grid give clues to the numbers in the four squares they touch. If a circle contains a number, then that is the difference between two numbers in diagonally adjacent cells. If it contains both a number and an addition sign (+), then that is the total of the numbers in diagonally adjacent cells. For example, "7+" means that when the numbers in two diagonally adjacent squares are added together, the answer is "7."

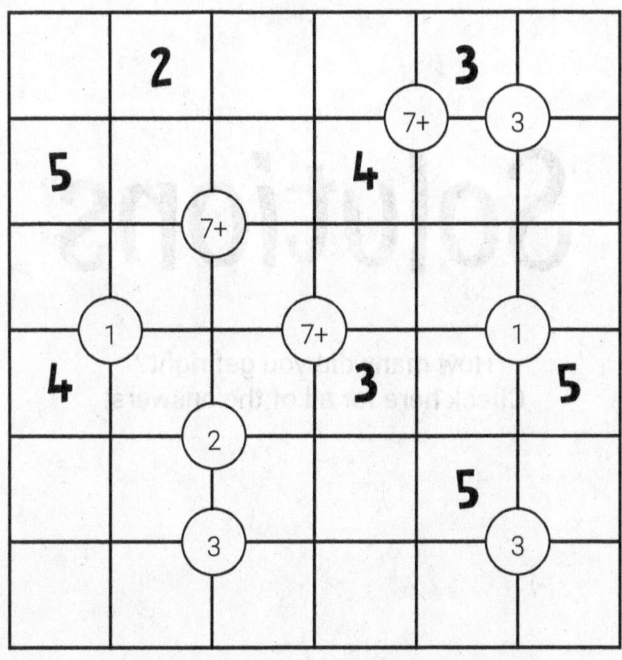

Solutions

How many did you get right?
Check here for all of the answers!

Solutions!

Page 3

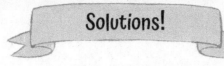

4	2	1	3
1	3	4	2
2	1	3	4
3	4	2	1

2	1	3	4
3	4	1	2
4	3	2	1
1	2	4	3

3	4	2	1
2	1	3	4
1	2	4	3
4	3	1	2

1	2	4	3
3	4	2	1
4	1	3	2
2	3	1	4

Page 4

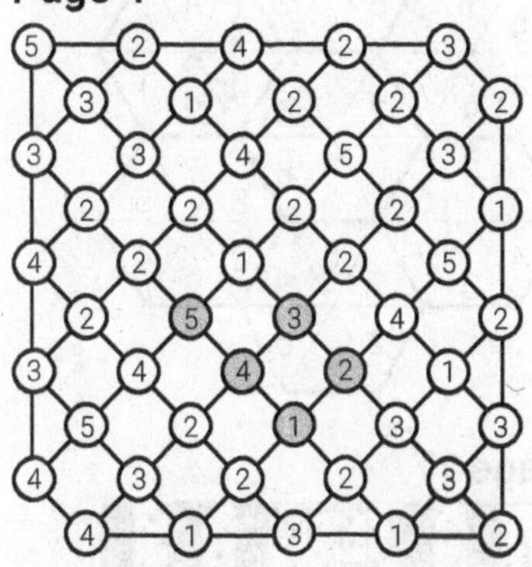

Page 5

14: The sequence is the previous number plus one, then that number plus two, then that number plus one, then that number plus two, repeated.
55: Add the two previous numbers to get the next each time.

Page 6

35
Four numbers (1, 5, 7, and 35) divide exactly into 35.

Page 7

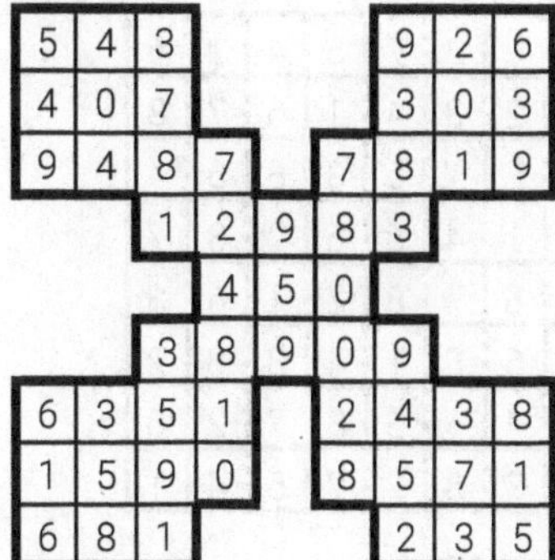

Page 8

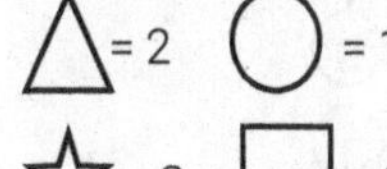

Page 9

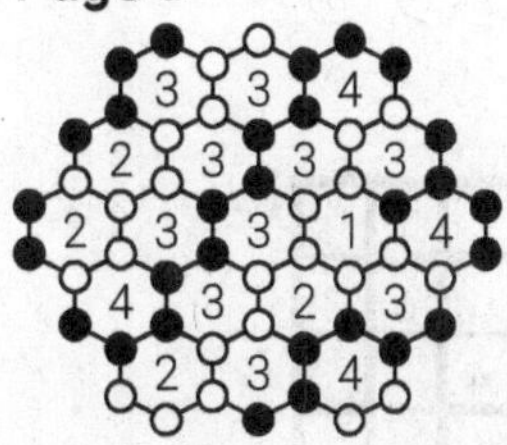

Page 10

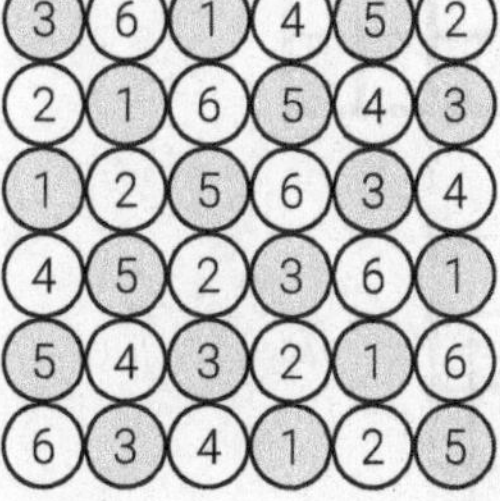

Solutions!

Page 11

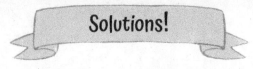

3	8	2	7	5	4	1	6
5	2	3	4	1	6	7	8
2	7	1	6	3	8	5	4
8	1	4	5	6	2	3	7
4	5	7	8	2	1	6	3
7	6	5	1	4	3	8	2
1	4	6	3	8	7	2	5
6	3	8	2	7	5	4	1

Page 12

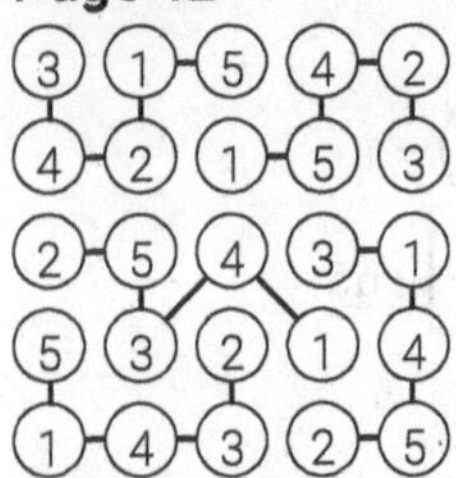

Page 13

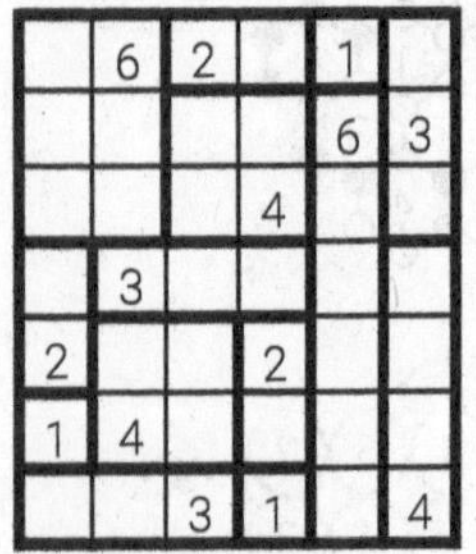

Page 14

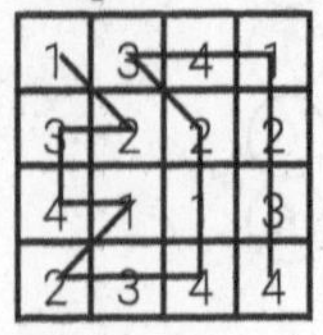

Page 15

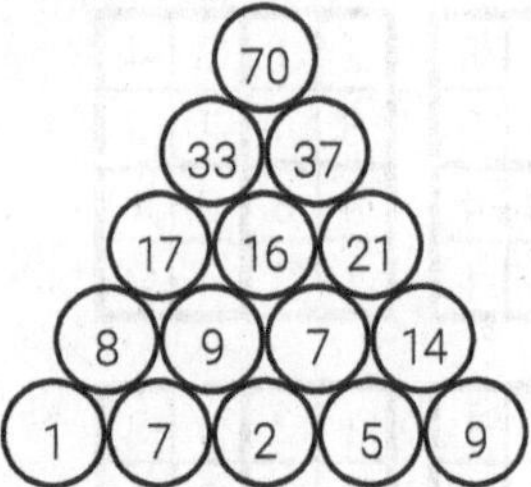

Page 16

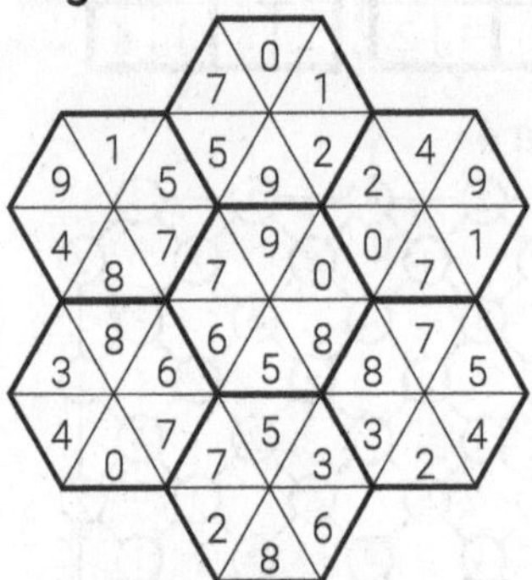

Page 17

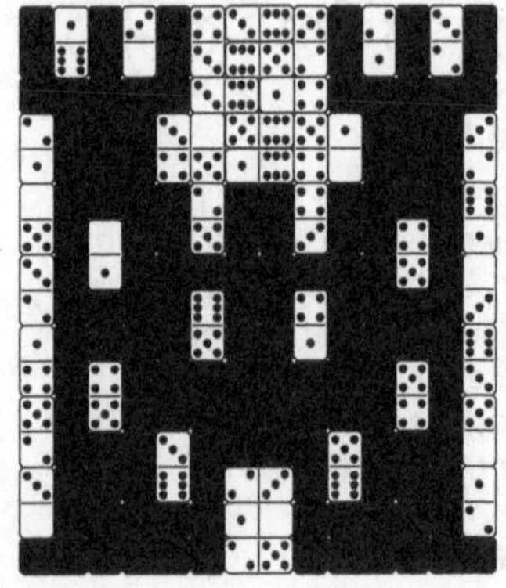

Solutions!

Page 18

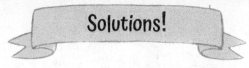

28
Six numbers (1, 2, 4, 7, 14, and 28) divide exactly into 28.

Page 19

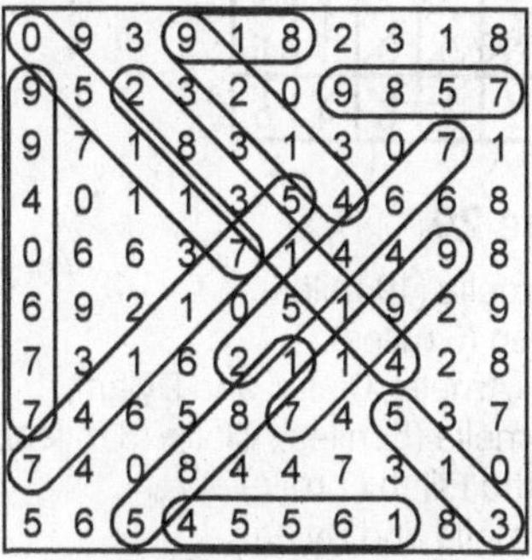

Page 20

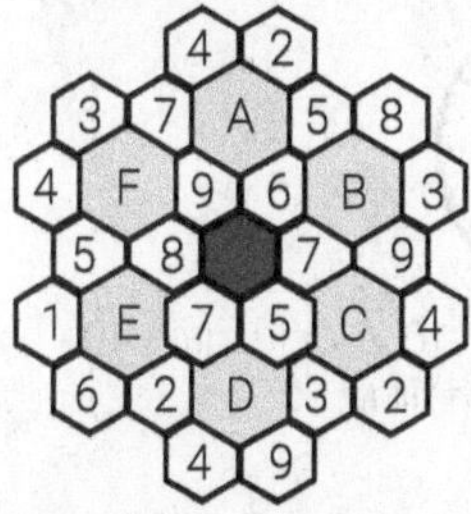

Page 21

The pairs are:
A and O, 2 x 8 = 16
B and I, 11 x 4 = 44
C and M, 10 x 10 = 100
D and K, 3 x 7 = 21
E and P, 7 x 5 = 35
F and L, 9 x 11 = 99
G and N, 8 x 6 = 48
H and J, 4 x 12 = 48
Two answers are the same:
G and N, and H and J.

Page 22

	11	8	17	3	5	12	6
7	18	15	24	10	12	19	13
9	20	17	26	12	14	21	15
4	15	12	21	7	9	16	10
8	19	16	25	11	13	20	14
2	13	10	19	5	7	14	8
16	27	24	33	19	21	28	22
10	21	18	27	13	15	22	16

Page 23

2	5	4	1	3	6
3	6	1	5	2	4
4	3	6	2	1	5
1	2	5	6	4	3
6	1	3	4	5	2
5	4	2	3	6	1

4	5	2	6	1	3
3	6	1	4	5	2
5	3	4	1	2	6
1	2	6	5	3	4
2	4	5	3	6	1
6	1	3	2	4	5

Page 24

1	3	5	2	4
3	4	1	5	2
5	2	4	1	3
2	1	3	4	5
4	5	2	3	1

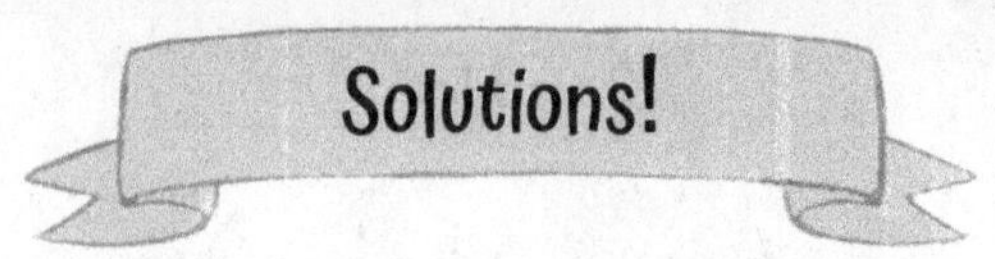

Page 25

D, H, and P
The total on each is 12:
D: 3 + 4 + 5 = 12
H: 1 + 5 + 6 = 12
P: 2 + 4 + 6 = 12

Page 26

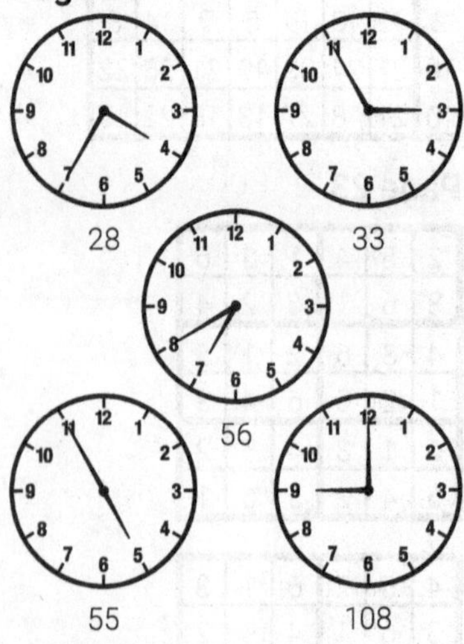

Page 27

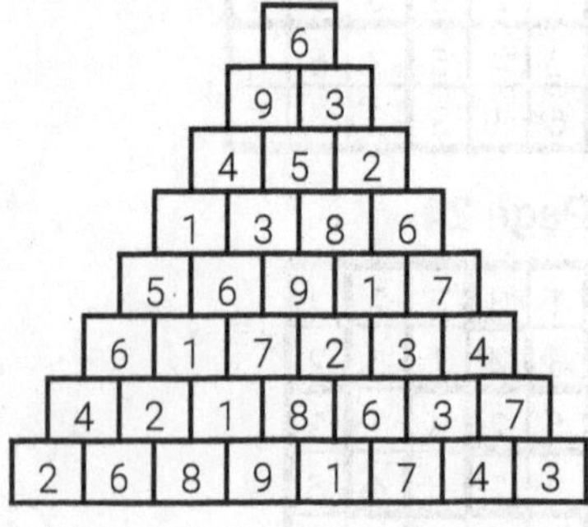

Page 28

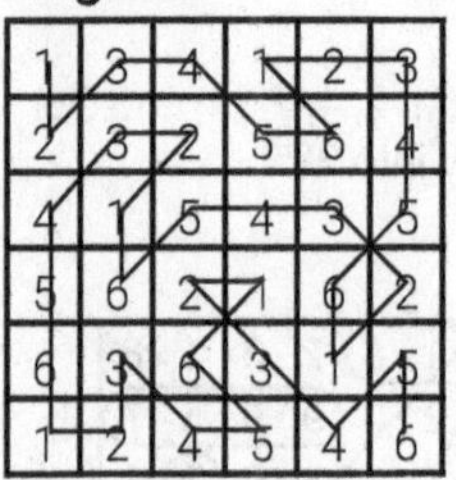

Page 29

1—Amelia (19 miles)
2—Ben (6 miles)
3—3 (Amelia, Claire, and Dylan)
4—Amelia (5 miles), Claire (3 miles), and Elijah (1 mile)
5—Amelia and Dylan

Page 30

The time is 6:10. Clocks gain 40 minutes each time.

Page 31

15	16	11	10	9	31	32
14	17	12	8	7	33	30
18	13	3	5	6	29	34
19	20	2	4	28	27	35
21	23	24	1	26	37	36
22	48	46	25	43	40	38
49	47	45	44	42	41	39

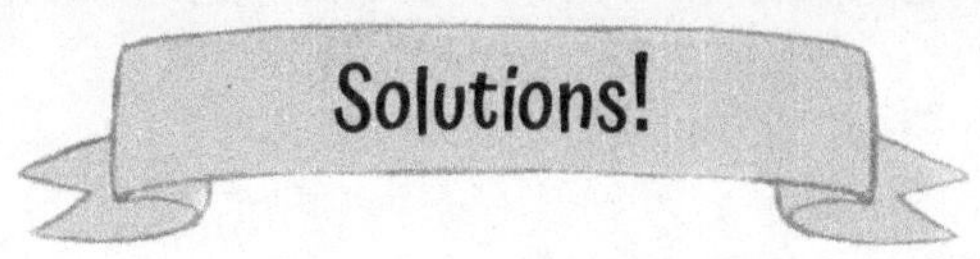

Page 32

A—24 (First add 3, then add 2 to the result, then add 3, then 2, etc.)
B—108 (The numbers are part of the 12 times table in reverse order.)
C—139 (Add the first two numbers to get the third, then the second and third to get the fourth, then the third and fourth to get the fifth, and so on.)
D—28 (The number between each two numbers increases by two each time: 1 + 2 = 3, then 3 + 3 = 6, 6 + 4 = 10, 10 + 5 = 15, and so on.)
E—96 (Each number is double the previous number.)
F—55 (First add 6, then add 8, then add 10, then add 12, then add 14, then add 16.)

Page 33

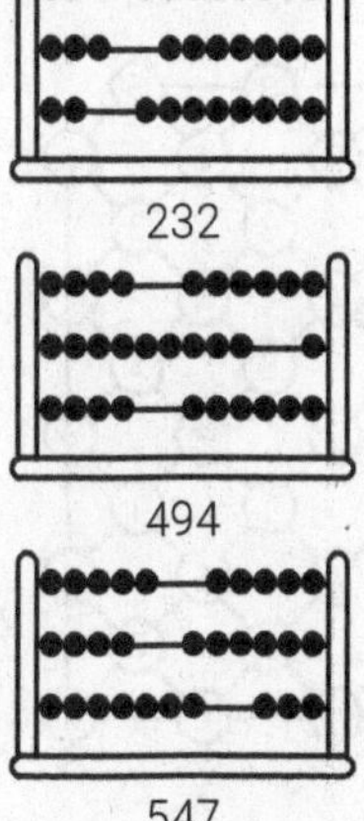

232

494

547

Page 34

2	5	2	4	4
2	5	2	4	4
5	5	5	3	3
2	4	1	3	2
2	4	4	4	2

Page 35

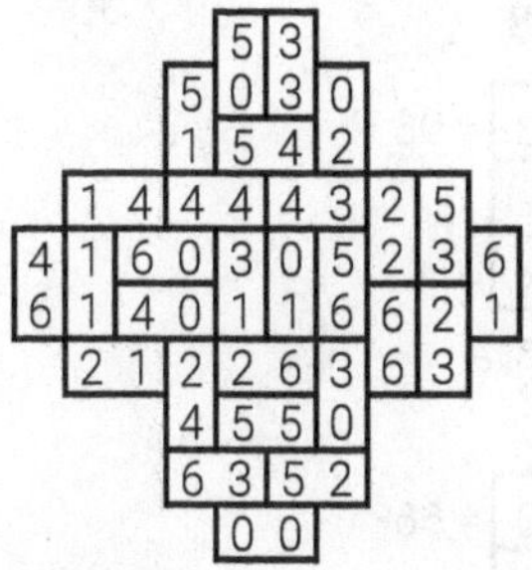

Page 36

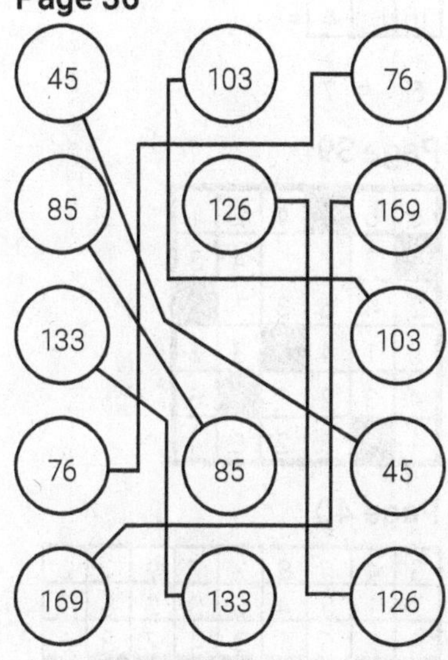

Solutions!

Page 37

	1	4		6	5
1	3	5	6		2
	6		4	5	1
6		1	5	2	3
4	5		2		6
	2	6	1	3	

Page 38

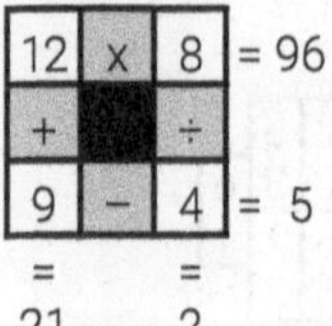

22	x	3	= 66
−		+	
16	÷	4	= 4
=		=	
6		7	

Page 39

3	5		4	2	1
	2	1	5	4	3
2	4	5	3	1	
5	1	4		3	2
4	3	2	1		5
1		3	2	5	4

Page 40

3	4	5	8	2	7	9	1	6
7	1	6	4	5	3	2	8	9
8	2	5	1	9	4	7	3	6
18	7	16	13	16	14	18	12	21

Page 41

1	2	3	1	2	5	4
2	1	4	2	5	1	3
1	3	2	1	4	3	2
4	5	1	3	1	4	1
1	2	3	1	2	1	5
2	1	5	4	1	2	3
3	4	2	5	3	1	4

Page 42

3	6	1	4	5	7	2
1	3	2	7	4	5	6
7	1	6	5	3	2	4
4	7	3	2	1	6	5
5	4	7	6	2	3	1
2	5	4	3	6	1	7
6	2	5	1	7	4	3

Page 43

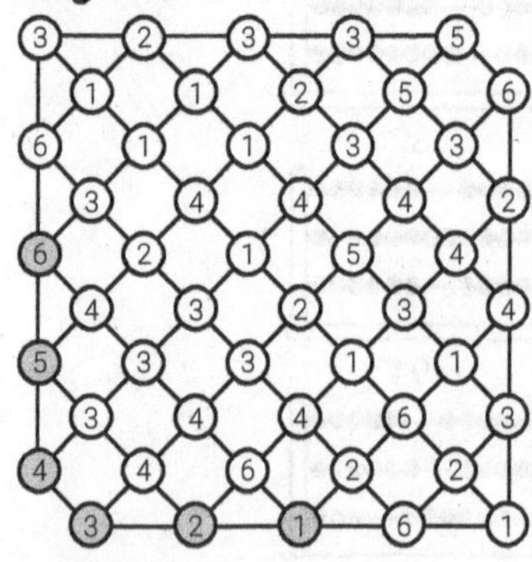

Page 44

44

Six numbers (1, 2, 4, 11, 22, and 44) divide exactly into 44.

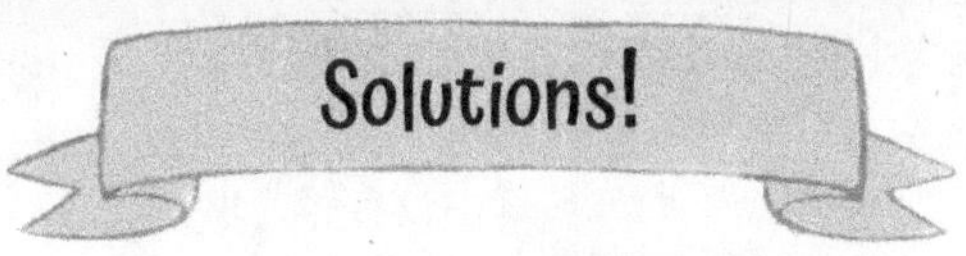

Page 45

24
Start City: 20 passengers got on,
Station A: 20 − 8 = 12. 12 + 3 = 15,
Station B: 15 − 3 = 12. 12 + 6 = 18,
Station C: 18 − 11 = 7. 7 + 5 = 12,
Station D: 12 − 9 = 3. 3 + 4 = 7,
Station E: 7 − 2 = 5. 5 + 7 = 12,
Station F: 12 − 4 = 8. 8 + 16 = 24,
Hometown: 24 passengers got off.

Page 46

Left column:
8 + 9 = 17
17 − 3 = 14
14 x 2 = 28
28 − 6 = 22
22 x 3 = 66

Right column:
15 − 8 = 7
7 x 3 = 21
21 + 4 = 25
25 x 4 = 100
100 − 20 = 80

Page 47

2	1	4	3	2	3	4	1
3	4	2	1	4	1	3	2
2	1	4	2	3	4	1	3
4	3	2	1	4	3	2	1
1	2	3	4	1	2	3	4
3	4	1	3	2	1	4	2
1	2	3	4	3	2	1	4
4	3	1	2	1	4	2	3

Page 48

13 (1 + 1 + 1 + 2 + 5 + 2 + 1)

3 | 37 → 12 r = 1
4 | 37 → 9 r = 1
8 | 37 → 4 r = 5
6 | 37 → 6 r = 1
2 | 37 → 18 r = 1
5 | 37 → 7 r = 2
7 | 37 → 5 r = 2

Page 49

21	19	8	3	15
9	7	22	19	9
15	6	10	20	15
12	13	16	13	12
9	21	10	11	15

Page 50

Add one triangle to the bottom scale, so both sides weigh 17.

△ = 8   ○ = 7

☆ = 2   □ = 5

Page 51

A = 1/4, B = 1/8, C = 1/16, D = 1/2, E = 3/8, F = 5/8.

Page 52

Page 53

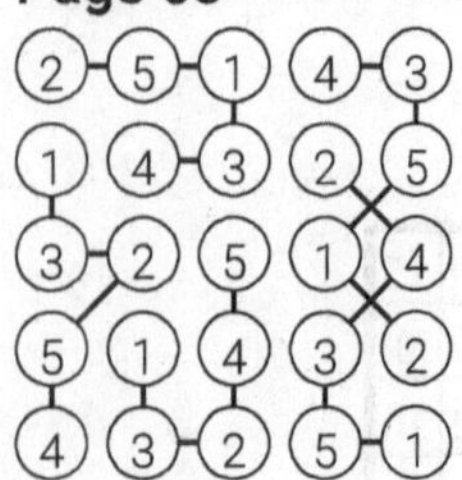

Page 54

These are the moves:
5, 7/39, 40, 44, 47, 53, 58, 60, 61, 65/20, 23, 29, 34, 36, 37/76, 80, 79, 77, 80, 80, 81.

Page 55

		3		6	
	6		2		
2		4			
	3			1	5
	4			6	

Page 56

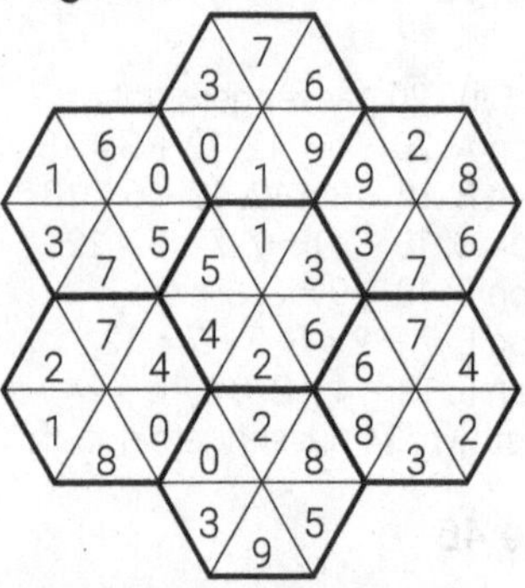

Page 57

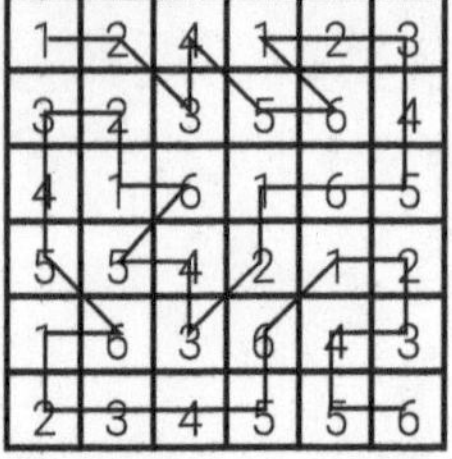

Page 58

3	63	1	28	52	12	96	39	7
16	15	37	44	27	81	22	51	38
50	48	72	42	93	35	5	69	9
8	25	71	40	11	20	98	46	6
26	10	72	57	51	64	14	29	33
43	84	6	2	21	30	90	45	78
21	60	17	49	13	53	31	61	4
9	32	41	87	54	66	36	15	47
36	75	18	48	19	23	34	99	3

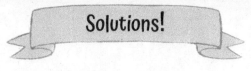

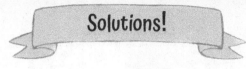

Solutions!

Page 59

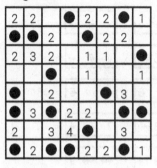

2	2		●	2	2	●	1
●	●	2		●	2	2	
2	3	2		1	1		●
		●		1			1
●		2			●	3	
●	3	●	2	2		●	●
2		3	4	●		3	
●	2	●	●	2	2	●	1

Page 60

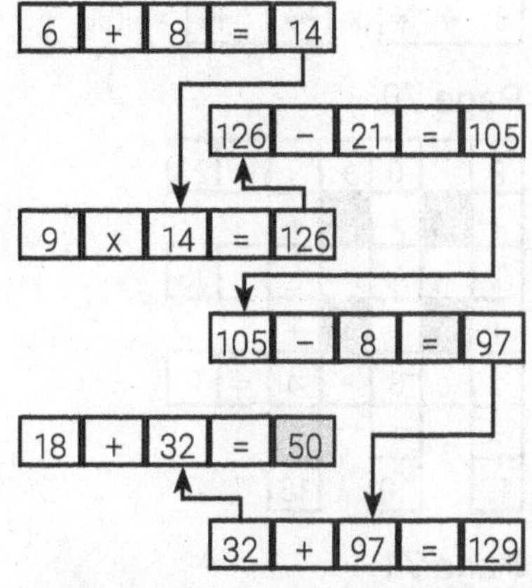

Page 61

	7	3	11	9	4	5
2	14	6	22	18	8	10
12	84	36	132	108	48	60
8	56	24	88	72	32	40
10	70	30	110	90	40	50
6	42	18	66	54	24	30
7	49	21	77	63	28	35

Page 62

22 ~~11~~ ~~9~~ + ~~34~~ 17 ~~6~~ = 39

9 ~~37~~ ~~45~~ + ~~20~~ ~~26~~ 43 = 52

~~19~~ 5 ~~4~~ + 18 ~~1~~ ~~10~~ = 23

~~42~~ ~~16~~ 41 + ~~24~~ 32 ~~47~~ = 73

~~36~~ ~~32~~ 15 + ~~20~~ ~~4~~ 31 = 46

25 ~~14~~ ~~30~~ + 49 ~~8~~ ~~10~~ = 74

Page 63

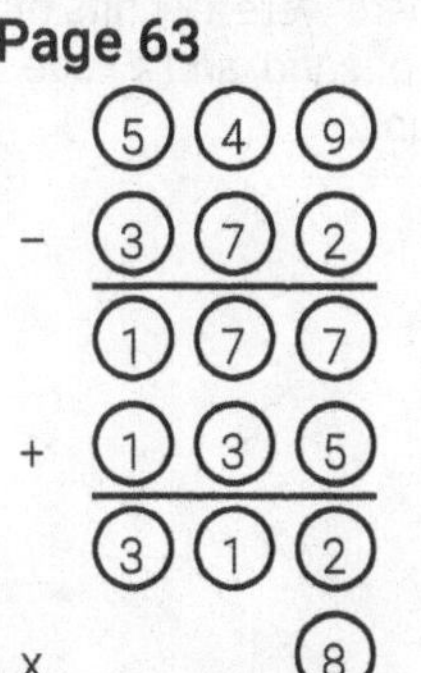

Page 64

1	2	1	3	2	1	5
3	1	2	1	4	2	3
1	3	1	4	1	3	1
2	1	4	2	5	1	2
4	5	2	3	1	2	4
1	2	3	1	2	4	3
3	4	1	2	3	1	2

Solutions!

Page 65

7	1	6	5	2	4	3
5	6	2	3	1	7	4
4	5	1	6	3	2	7
2	4	3	7	6	1	5
6	7	4	2	5	3	1
3	2	7	1	4	5	6
1	3	5	4	7	6	2

Page 66

The weight was 17 units. The vase and sand had not evaporated, just the water; so there were 12 units of water, one unit of sand, and a vase weighing four units.

Page 67

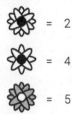

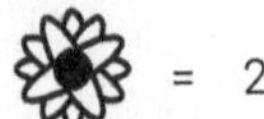 = 2

= 4

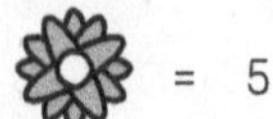 = 5

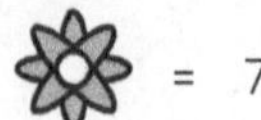 = 7

Page 68

347

The first digit is the number of sides that make up the shape on the left. The second digit is the number of sides that make up the shape on the right. The third digit is the total number of sides of both shapes.

Page 69

~~7~~ ~~8~~ 9 x 8 ~~7~~ ~~6~~ = 72

~~12~~ 16 ~~11~~ x 4 ~~7~~ ~~6~~ = 64

6 ~~7~~ ~~8~~ x ~~13~~ 14 ~~15~~ = 84

~~17~~ 13 ~~21~~ x 7 ~~5~~ ~~4~~ = 91

~~16~~ ~~12~~ 14 x ~~14~~ ~~10~~ 9 = 126

8 ~~4~~ ~~6~~ x ~~19~~ 17 ~~18~~ = 136

Page 70

8	+	6	+	9	=	23
+		+		+		
7	+	1	+	5	=	13
+		+		+		
2	+	3	+	4	=	9
=		=		=		
17		10		18		

Page 71

8	3	1	6	5	7	2	9	4
9	5	6	2	8	4	1	7	3
2	4	7	3	1	9	6	8	5
7	2	8	4	9	6	5	3	1
4	1	5	8	3	2	9	6	7
6	9	3	5	7	1	4	2	8
3	6	9	1	4	8	7	5	2
5	7	4	9	2	3	8	1	6
1	8	2	7	6	5	3	4	9

Solutions!

Page 72

Page 73

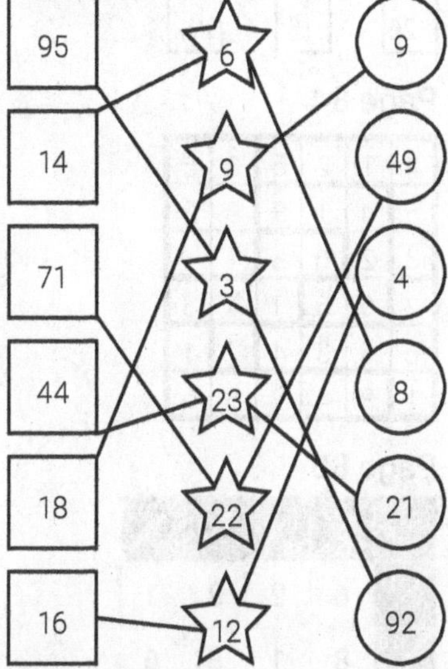

Page 74

2	4	1	3	2	1	5
1	2	3	4	1	2	3
3	1	2	1	3	1	4
4	3	1	2	1	4	2
1	2	4	3	2	5	1
2	1	3	1	4	2	3
3	4	5	2	3	1	2

Page 75

28

The numbers in each large square add up to 44.

Page 76

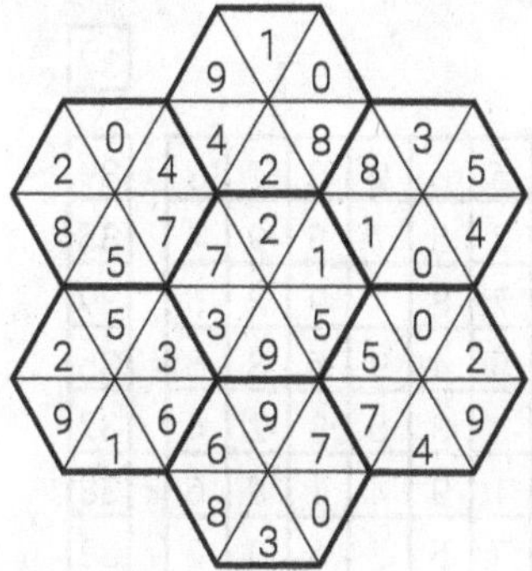

Page 77

2	1	3	5	4
3	2	4	1	5
4	3	5	2	1
5	4	1	3	2
1	5	2	4	3

Page 78

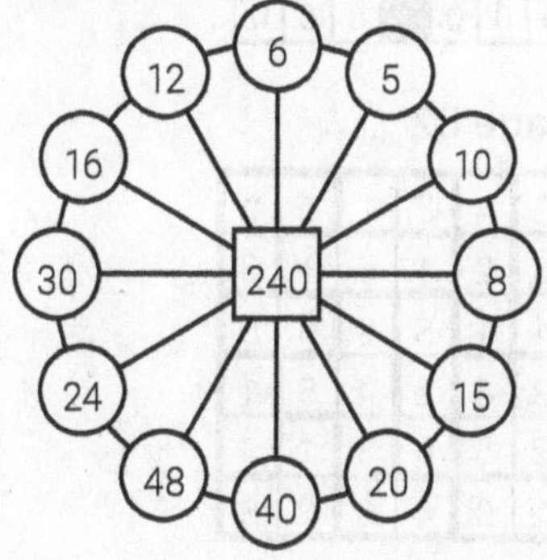

Page 79

A: 2:00 p.m.
B: 8:00 a.m.
C: 5:00 p.m.

Page 80

							37
1	5	6	9	8	7	3	39
3	2	5	7	5	9	4	35
6	7	8	1	9	2	6	39
1	5	4	9	6	3	8	36
7	8	3	5	8	2	4	37
9	1	9	4	1	8	6	38
3	7	5	7	6	3	2	33
30	35	40	42	43	34	33	38

Page 81

5	5	5		1	0	8
4		2	4	6		0
1	4	4		1	6	5
	0				4	
1	0	4		1	3	3
0		2	2	1		0
9	0	0		8	8	0

Page 82

5	4	3	1	6	2
6	2	1	5	4	3
4	1	5	2	3	6
3	6	2	4	5	1
2	5	6	3	1	4
1	3	4	6	2	5

Page 83

7	x	3	x	6	=	126
x		x		x		
2	x	5	x	8	=	80
x		x		x		
9	x	1	x	4	=	36
=		=		=		
126		15		192		

Page 84

4	1	2	6	3	5
5	4	1	3	6	2
3	2	6	5	1	4
2	6	5	1	4	3
6	5	3	4	2	1
1	3	4	2	5	6

Page 85

	14	38	38	7
12	6	2	3	1
20	8	1	5	6
	17	8	9	
	15 / 24	7	8	5
21	7	5	6	3
24	9	6	7	2
17	8	9		

Solutions!

Page 86

a) 15 x 2 = 30 + 13 = 43
b) 51 − 23 = 28 ÷ 2 = 14
c) 27 ÷ 9 = 3 x 5 = 15
d) 16 + 4 = 20 ÷ 4 = 5
e) 36 − 28 = 8 x 8 = 64
f) 42 ÷ 6 = 7 + 18 = 25

Page 87

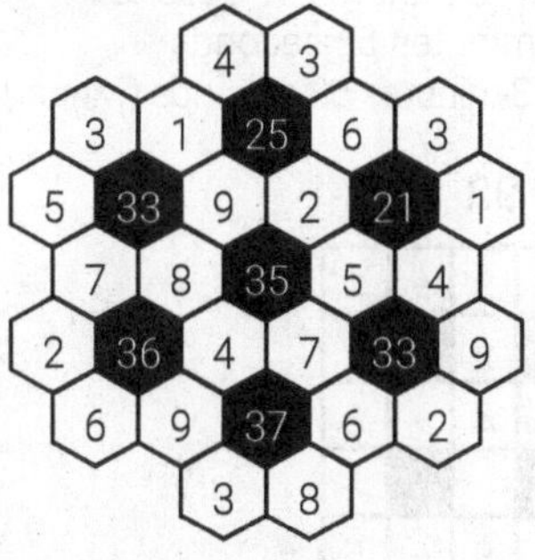

Page 88

176 and 18325 will not fit:

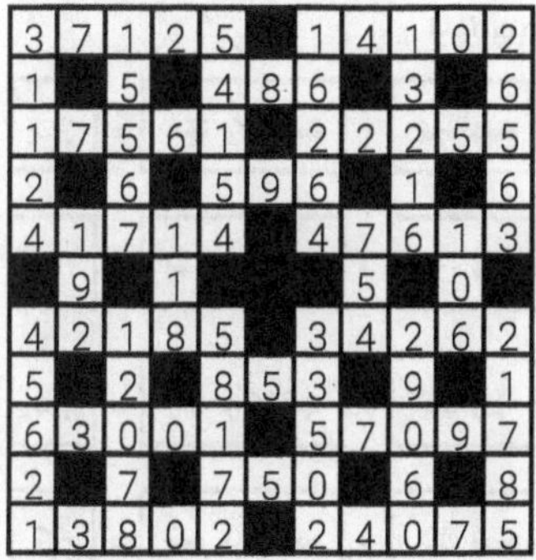

3	7	1	2	5		1	4	1	0	2
1		5		4	8	6		3		6
1	7	5	6	1		2	2	2	5	5
2		6		5	9	6		1		6
4	1	7	1	4		4	7	6	1	3
	9		1				5		0	
4	2	1	8	5		3	4	2	6	2
5		2		8	5	3		9		1
6	3	0	0	1		5	7	0	9	7
2		7		7	5	0		6		8
1	3	8	0	2		2	4	0	7	5

Page 89

9
The sum total of the numbers in the outer squares minus the number in the central square is 24.

Page 90

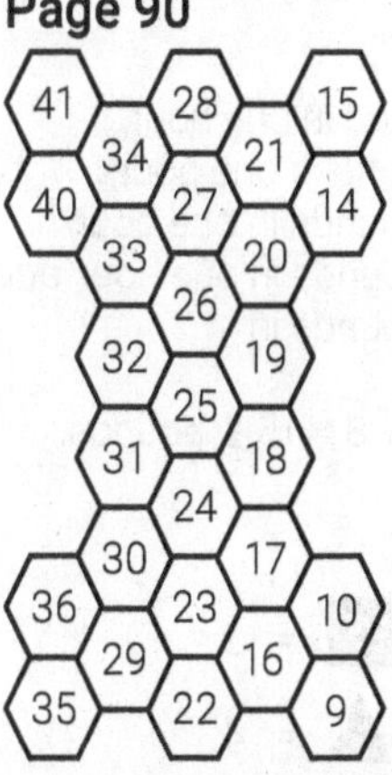

Page 91

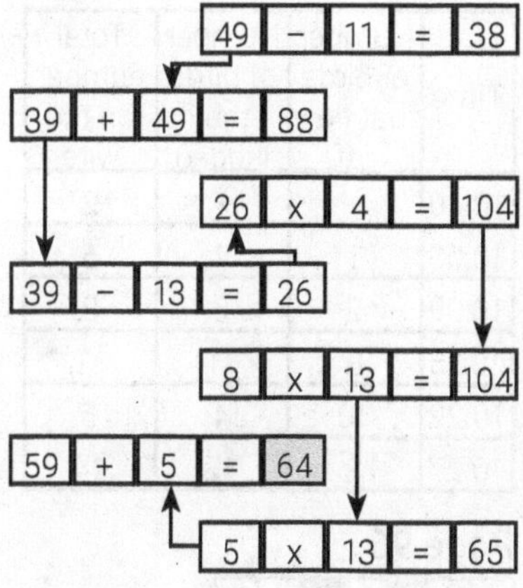

Page 92

14 pounds
Donny ate 2 pounds in one hour, Denny ate 4 pounds in one hour, and Danny ate 8 pounds in one hour:
2 + 4 + 8 = 14 pounds.

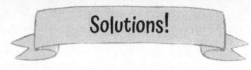

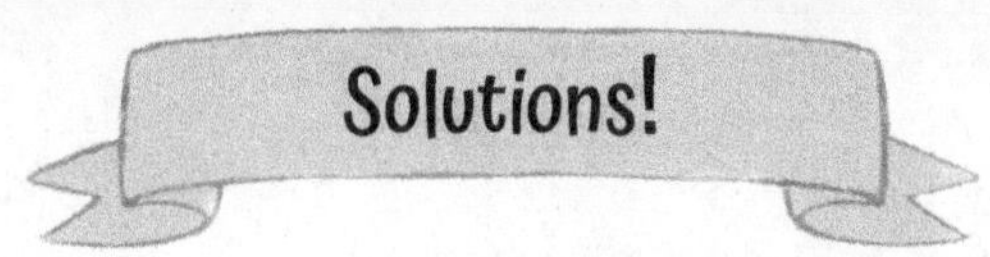

Page 93

1½ pounds
Dilly ate ½ pound in one hour,
Doris ate 1 pound in one hour,
Donny ate 2 pounds in one hour,
Denny ate 4 pounds in one hour, and
Danny ate 8 pounds in
one hour:
½ + 1 + 2 + 4 + 8 = 15½ pounds.

Page 94

● = 3 ■ = 2
★ = 8 ▲ = 4

Page 95

Time	Number of birds that flew off	Number of birds that landed	Total number on the wire
10:00	-	-	2
10:05	1	4	5
10:09	2	5	8
10:16	8	11	11
10:22	10	4	5
10:27	3	12	14

Page 96

6	6		7		4	2
0			3	9	1	
9		3	1	4		
5	3	4		1	0	9
		4	6	0		5
	2	9	9			4
6	2		9		6	4

Page 97

Runner	Lap 1	Lap 2	Lap 3	Lap 4	Total Time
Georgie	58	56	59	64	237
Hal	57	60	55	63	235
Indira	56	54	61	62	233

Georgie: 3 minutes 57 seconds
Hal: 3 minutes 55 seconds
Indira: 3 minutes 53 seconds (winner)

Page 98

7	−	3	÷	1	= 4
+		x		+	
9	x	4	÷	6	= 6
÷		−		−	
2	+	8	÷	5	= 2
=		=		=	
8		4		2	

Page 99

12 ~~13~~ ~~14~~	+	~~16~~ 22 ~~26~~	=	34
~~67~~ ~~65~~ 63	÷	~~9~~ 7 ~~8~~	=	9
~~47~~ 43 ~~49~~	-	~~17~~ ~~21~~ 19	=	24
~~36~~ ~~38~~ 44	+	~~15~~ 19 ~~17~~	=	63
8 ~~9~~ ~~4~~	x	~~6~~ ~~12~~ 7	=	56
~~88~~ 84 ~~72~~	÷	~~7~~ 6 ~~8~~	=	14

Page 100

1	3	5	4	2
5	2	3	1	4
3	4	2	5	1
2	1	4	3	5
4	5	1	2	3

Page 101

Left column:
28 ÷ 2 = 14
14 x 3 = 42
42 − 15 = 27
27 + 39 = 66
66 ÷ 3 = 22

Right column:
28 x 5 = 140
140 ÷ 7 = 20
20 + 57 = 77
77 ÷ 11 = 7
7 + 83 = 90

Page 102

3	3	4	4	4	4
3	5	5	5	1	2
2	5	6	6	6	2
2	5	2	2	6	3
3	3	4	6	6	3
1	3	4	4	4	3

Page 103

The numbers are on the white petals:
7 x 10 x 13 = 910
The other numbers multiply together as follows:
5 x 8 x 11 = 440
6 x 9 x 12 = 648

Page 104

3	9	4	5	8	7	1	6	2
2	8	1	4	9	6	5	7	3
6	5	7	2	1	3	8	4	9
4	2	8	6	3	5	7	9	1
5	7	9	1	4	2	3	8	6
1	3	6	8	7	9	4	2	5
9	4	5	7	2	1	6	3	8
7	1	3	9	6	8	2	5	4
8	6	2	3	5	4	9	1	7

Page 105

Answer = 83

Page 106

C—Reading from left to right, all odd numbers in the same position in each grid increase by 6, and even numbers in the same position in each grid increase by 4.

Solutions!

Page 107

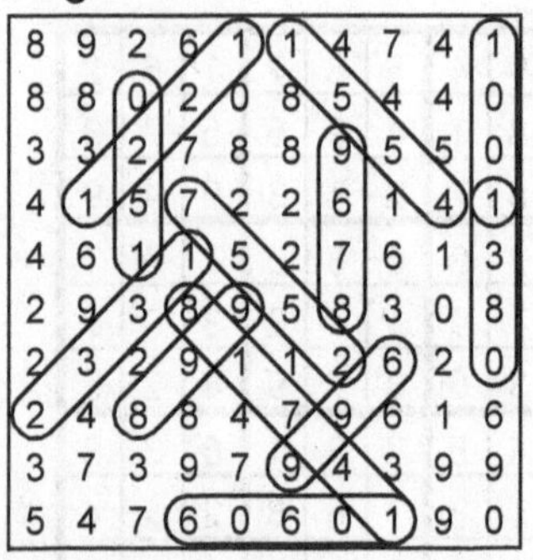

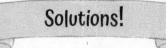

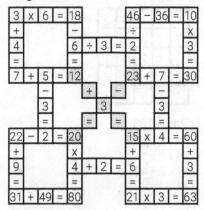

232 + 989 = 1,221
678 + 876 = 1,554
1,020 − 22 = 998
38 x 40 = 1,520
3,776 + 3,776 = 7,552
10,010 ÷ 10 = 1,001
345 x 4 = 1,380
9,743 − 974 = 8,769
332 + 332 + 332 = 996
4,906 x 3 = 14,718
864 + 468 = 1,332
63,636 ÷ 6 = 10,606

Page 108

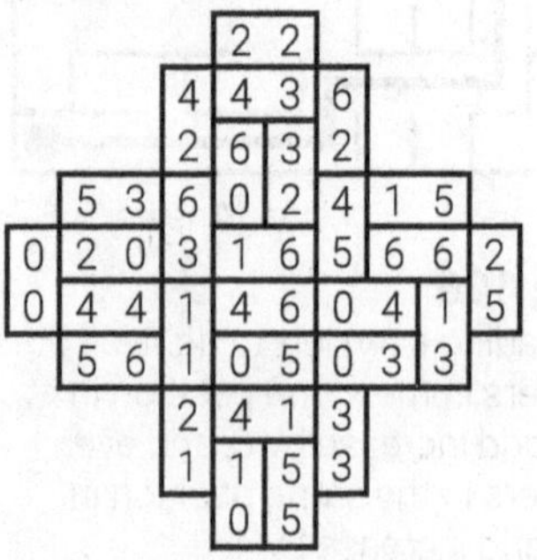

Page 109

3	x	6	=	18				46	−	36	=	10
+				−				÷				x
4				6	÷	3	=	2				3
=				=				=				=
7	+	5	=	12				23	+	7	=	30
		−			+		−			−		
		3				3				3		
		=			=		=			=		
22	−	2	=	20				15	x	4	=	60
+				x				+				+
9				4	+	2	=	6				3
=				=				=				=
31	+	49	=	80				21	x	3	=	63

Page 110

14	15	12	19	10	9	7	5
16	13	18	11	20	8	4	6
29	17	25	24	22	21	51	3
30	28	34	26	23	50	52	2
31	33	27	35	47	49	53	1
41	32	36	46	48	63	55	54
42	40	45	37	64	62	59	56
43	44	39	38	61	60	57	58

Page 111

1	2	5	6	3	4
5	3	2	4	1	6
2	5	4	1	6	3
4	1	6	3	2	5
6	4	3	2	5	1
3	6	1	5	4	2